MIDWEST HERITAGE

MIDWEST HERITAGE

BY JOHN DRURY

With Hundreds of Old Engravings

A. A. WYN, INC. NEW YORK

Designed by Flora Finn

CONTENTS

MIDWEST HERITAGE

ON "THE FATHER OF WATERS"

ALONG the foot of the wharf, like a row of monstrous wedding cakes, stand the great white steamboats, gaudy packets with tall stacks, out of which black smoke ascends to the summer sky. Bells are ringing. From the river comes the mournful sound of a steamer whistle. On the sunny wharf sweating Negro stevedores rush bales and barrels over gangways. Drays rattle on cobblestones. Beaux and belles, gay in beaver hats and crinolines, arrive in carriages. Above the rattle of the drays, the songs of the Negroes, the calls of coachmen, the chatter of men, women, and children can be heard the shouts of husky mates, the ringing of bells, the whine of deck winches.

Such was a typical summer afternoon on the Saint Louis levee just after the Civil War. Saint Louis was the principal metropolis on the upper reaches of the Mississippi.

Travelers were astonished at the magnitude and grandeur of the river. This was the era of such splendid big packets as the *Grand Republic, Aleck Scott, Grand Turk, Robert E. Lee,* and *Natchez.* The Mississippi and its two most important tributaries, the Ohio and Missouri, were in their heyday as highways of travel and transportation in mid-continental America.

And this was the period when Saint Louis stood supreme as the steamboat capital of the Western waters, when "floating palaces" from New Orleans, Natchez, Memphis, Louisville, and Cincinnati were lined up for miles along the Saint Louis levee, taking on and discharging cargoes and passengers.

The Mississippi steamboats were nothing less than the most gorgeous of palaces to a backwoodsman or an immigrant of the time. Sometimes five decks high, they were painted white with trimmings of green or other colors. And what trimmings! The decks, staterooms, railings, pilot-houses, and almost everything else were edged with the most intricate of scrollwork designs. Even the great semicircular boxes housing the paddle wheels flaunted landscapes, sunbursts, and other ornate pictures. Fore and aft, on tall staffs, floated the national colors and house flags, and the tops of the sky-reaching smokestacks were cut to resemble outspraying fern plants. An object of particular prominence on the top, or "Texas," deck, and one that received especial attention from the hand of the decorator, was the pilot-house. Almost all of us remember, with a warm glow, our first reading of the experiences and adventures of "Mark Twain" as a pilot in such a glass-enclosed house on the Texas deck.

No less decorative than the exterior of a Mississippi packet was its interior. In fact,

here was even more luxuriance of ornamental detail. The *salon* was like a magnificent hotel ballroom, only three or four times longer than an ordinary hotel ballroom From the white ceiling, ornamented with rosettes and elaborate cornices, hung crystal chandeliers of the most entrancing designs. From the ceiling, too, through colored skylights, came, of a sunny afternoon on the river, tints of red, green, and blue.

In these resplendent cabins Southern planters and Saint Louis merchants, with their ladies in hoop skirts, dined on the choicest of viands, served on fine Haviland china, while soft music from a stringed orchestra lent romantic charm to the scene. And afterward, the *salon* was cleared of tables and the orchestra struck up dance music, and the passengers danced the polka, cotillion, waltz, minuet, and mazurka. But there were other passengers on board who did not enjoy the glittering chandeliers, the

SAINT LOUIS LEVEE

STEAMBOAT FIRE, SAINT LOUIS

savory food, the service of white-coated Negro waiters. These were the backwoodsmen, the frontier settlers, the immigrants, they and their wives and children. These passengers could only afford passage on the first, or boiler, deck, but they could hear the strains of the *salon* music and get some pleasure from it. Meanwhile, a well-groomed "black leg," or gambler, might be mingling sociably with the throngs.

All was not beer and skittles on the Mississippi in those grandiose days. Steamboat travel had its dangers. In addition to steamboat explosions, which were quite common on the Western waters in pioneer times, the destruction of vessels by fire while tied to their moorings was a frequent occurrence. One such catastrophe came to the Saint Louis levee early on a July morning in 1856 and was of such a spectacular nature as to attract thousands of persons to both banks of the Mississippi. The fire started in the cabin of the steamer *Saint Clair,* which was tied to the upper landing. The flames spread to the *Paul Anderson* and soon both steamers were roaring infernos. Then other boats, including the luxurious *Southerner,* were in flames. The early-morning sky was black with smoke, and flying sparks sizzled on the water in all directions. Fire engines were rushed down the levee to the burning ships, but the conflagration was out of control. As more and more spectators gathered, swelling to thousands, the great fire roared to its peak, devouring one ship after another, and then burned itself out.

At this time, Saint Louis was a commercial and mercantile city of first rank in the Midwest, deriving much of its prosperity not only from the steamboat trade but also from the fur trade and as an outfitting station for wagon trains about to set out for the Far West. In the beginning a small French trading post built by a party of workmen under René Auguste Chouteau, then but fifteen years old, Saint Louis grew as flat-boat and keelboat traffic on the Mississippi increased and more settlers came. From a contented and easygoing village of French *habitants* called "Carondelet," which had appeared around the trading post, it soon expanded into a thriving town of American fur agents, merchants, farmers, flatboatmen, land speculators, and adventurers. With the arrival of the steamboat era, Southern planters, Creoles from New Orleans, and others from the cotton country appeared in Saint Louis, built homes with galleries, planted gardens, and introduced an atmosphere of Southern leisure. Much of this prosperity and elegance, of course, was built on a

CATHEDRAL OF SAINT LOUIS OF FRANCE

foundation of inexpensive Negro labor.

From the very first, there was a sizable element of Catholics in Saint Louis, originating from the early French settlers. Standing today as one of the city's most revered and historic landmarks is the Old Cathedral of Saint Louis of France. On Walnut Street, between Second and Third Streets, this Greek Revival edifice of yellowing limestone was built more than a hundred years ago, before the day of the "floating palaces."

Possessing a special indulgence granted by Pope Gregory XVI, having in its in-

terior three old oil paintings said to have been presented to the church by Louis XVIII, and echoing at mass to the tones of an ancient bell made in part of two hundred Spanish silver dollars, the Old Cathedral of Saint Louis of France will continue to remain on its original site and will form one of the principal sights in the new Thomas Jefferson Memorial Plaza.

No longer standing is the first house, aside from a few log cabins, to be erected in Saint Louis, the Chouteau Mansion. This was the home of the founder of Saint Louis. A native of New Orleans, René Auguste Chouteau designed his house in the Creole style, with the roof flaring outward to form a spacious gallery. It was in 1764 that the youthful Chouteau, a fur trader, decided on the future site of Saint Louis as a suitable fur-trading post and at once began the construction of his house. It was not really his house at first, being built for his senior, Pierre Laclede. But with the death of Laclede some few years later, the dwelling came into the possession of Chouteau and was occupied by him thereafter.

This mansion, which stood near the Old Saint Louis Cathedral and fronted on the river, was originally a one-story building. As there were few white laborers at the time, much of the work on it was done by Indians. All planking used in the house was

CHOUTEAU MANSION

hand-hewn out of solid timbers, since there were no sawmills or saw pits in the vicinity. It was Chouteau who added the second story and galleries. All during this time the square on which the mansion stood was bordered by a stone wall, which, with its portholes, formed something of a defense against Indian attack. Here, with his brother, Jean Pierre, René Auguste Chouteau directed a far-flung trading activity in furs, an activity that was responsible for the founding of Saint Louis.

René Auguste Chouteau, with John B. C. Lucas, donated a square of land in early Saint Louis for the erection of a courthouse. The building was constructed and served until 1839, when work was begun on a two-story, domed edifice of stone on the same site, and this became the pride of the river metropolis during steamboating days. Still standing, it is now one of the most treasured of the city's relics. This historic courthouse will also become part of the new Thomas Jefferson Memorial Plaza. Few buildings in the Midwest are associated with so many historical events and personages as is the old Saint Louis Courthouse. And during all the glorious days of the Mississippi packets, the dome of this courthouse was a familiar sight to river pilots.

From the east entrance of this building Henry Clay sold real estate in 1847; in the rotunda were held meetings of citizens to raise troops for the Mexican War, and later some of these troops were quartered here; it is recorded that in this building Ulysses S. Grant gave legal freedom to his only slave; in 1849 there was held in the rotunda the first national railroad convention in America, at which Stephen A. Douglas served as chairman and Thomas Hart Benton closed his eloquent plea for a transcontinental railroad with the words: "There is the East. There is India." Of all the events that oc-

MEETING AT SAINT LOUIS COURTHOUSE

curred in the old Saint Louis Courthouse, however, none was of more far-reaching importance than the famous Dred Scott trial, a contributing factor to the Civil War.

As in the past, this courthouse again became a rallying point of citizens on a Sunday afternoon in 1856, only this time the gathering was even more tense. On that Sunday afternoon citizens in carriages, buggies, wagons, and on horseback and afoot, came to the rotunda to attend a public meeting on the "Kansas situation." They were alarmed because Saint Louis was suffering a loss of business as an outfitting station for anti-slavery Easterners on their way to the new Territory of Kansas. These Easterners were now avoiding Saint Louis; they feared hos-

SAINT LOUIS SHOT TOWER

tile proslavery Southerners. In view of this situation, and in an atmosphere charged with strong feeling, the courthouse mass meeting took place. Resolutions were passed calling on the Federal Government to subdue armed bands, both proslavery "Border Ruffians," as they were called, and antislavery Kansas settlers, along the then bloody Kansas-Missouri border.

At this time, there was another important landmark in Saint Louis besides the courthouse. This was the Saint Louis Shot Tower, which rose to a height of seventy-six feet at the north end of town. A large portion of the shot used by the frontiersmen was made in the Saint Louis Shot Tower. In the 1850s three hundred and eighty-three pigs of lead were converted into shot daily inside the tower, missiles that made possible such savory "grub" for settlers in the early Midwestern clearings as roast duck and venison steaks.

For many years Saint Louis was the northern terminus of river traffic, with New Orleans the southern. After the Civil War, however, more and more palatial packets appeared on the Mississippi above Saint Louis, serving bustling river towns in Illinois, Iowa, Wisconsin, and Minnesota. This reach of "The Father of Waters" is far more picturesque and rugged than the lower reach, with magnificent bluffs on either bank standing out dramatically at dawn or sunset. There became popular at this time "The Fashionable Tour" of the Upper Mississippi. Not only Easterners from New York, Boston, and such cities, and even visiting Englishmen, but well-to-do Southerners from all parts of Dixieland went on the Fashionable Tour, enjoying the new scenery and slow pace of the river voyage as far as Fort Snelling and the city it guarded, Saint Paul.

Just above Alton, Illinois, is that most ancient and awesome of Mississippi River wonders the Piasa Bird. It is a large painting of a weird birdlike animal on the Illinois bluff, which at this point has a smooth surface. When first observed, however, by the French explorers Father Marquette and Louis Jolliet, on their memorable voyage down the Mississippi in 1673, the Piasa Bird was more than one bird. Father Marquette wrote in his *Journal*: "As we were descending the river we saw high rocks with hideous monsters painted on them. . . . They are as large as a calf, with head and horns like a goat; their eyes red; beard like a tiger; and a face like a man's. . . . They are painted red, green, and black."

But when the pioneer Saint Louis illustrator, J. C. Wild, saw this legendary sight in the 1840s, it was but one bird. This is his version: "Its [the bluff's] summit is sparsely studded with dwarf cedars, and it presents a craggy and jagged front, with the exception of a space of about fifty feet by forty, which is smooth and even. On this space is emblazoned the figure of a hybridous animal, having a head resembling that of a fox, from which protrude large horns or antlers; its back is supplied with wings, and it has a long curling tail, and four feet, or rather, four huge claws." Anyway, whatever its form or number, the Piasa Bird, sometimes called "The Thunder Bird," was an object anciently feared by the Indians. Their legend tells that the Piasa Bird was a thing of evil that lived in a cave here and would swoop down on the waters of the Mississippi and carry off Indians, canoes and all. It was not until an Illinois chief and twenty of his warriors destroyed it with poisoned arrows, according to the legend, that the Piasa Bird menace was removed.

Some miles north of the Thunder Bird lies a Missouri town that was destined to become known throughout the world in the twentieth century. It is Hannibal, where Mark Twain grew to manhood and where he derived inspiration for *Tom Sawyer, Huckleberry Finn,* and *Life on the Mississippi.*

In the late 1850s, Hannibal was an alert and flourishing river town, quite a contrast to the "little white town drowsing in the sunlight of a summer morning," as Mark Twain described the village of his boyhood. This change was brought about by the railroad, which ended the great days of the Mississippi packets. In 1856 the first train of the Hannibal and Saint Joseph Railroad—the first railroad to cross Missouri—moved out of Mark Twain's boyhood town and thus began a new era for the once sleepy river village. Curiously enough, it was young Clemens' father, John Marshall Clemens, a struggling lawyer, who had called a meeting of citizens in Hannibal to discuss the build-

PIASA BIRD ROCK

[15]

HANNIBAL

"STEAMBOAT A-COMIN'!"

LEARNING THE RIVER

ing of the Hannibal and Saint Joe Railroad.

But in the days of young Sam Clemens, the arrival of a steamboat caused great excitement in the little white town, drowsing there on its riverbank under a hot July sun. With a wharfside shout of "Steamboat a-comin'!" the town suddenly came alive. Not only the clerks in the water-front stores and the Negroes on the sunny levee but the "fragrant" town drunkard, too, would rush down to the water's edge to watch the arrival of the big white steamboat, with its polished brass, tall smokestacks, and big, dripping paddle wheels. Sam Clemens watched that majestic personage the pilot, high up on the Texas deck, and determined to become just such a personage when he grew up.

And this, as we all know, he succeeded in doing. After Clemens left Hannibal at the age of eighteen, he served as a journeyman printer in various cities and then, somehow inevitably, drifted back to the river of his boyhood, where he eventually became a steamboat pilot. As an apprentice in the wheelhouse of a Mississippi steamer, however, young Clemens did not always have smooth sailing. There were times when a snag in the channel up ahead, or a foggy morning on the river, or perhaps one of those fierce thunderstorms so common to the region, threw him off his course and brought down on his head the wrath of his master, Mr. Horace Bixby. However, he pulled through his apprenticeship.

Among all the other fascinating matters on river life that Mark Twain discusses in *Life on the Mississippi*, not the least interesting is his description of steamboat races on the river. The greatest river race of all time was the one between the *Robert E. Lee* and the *Natchez*. Bets were made all the way from log-cabin clearings in the Midwest and South to the most exclusive clubs in London and Paris. Nothing like it was ever staged

THE *Robert E. Lee*

before and both banks of the Mississippi from New Orleans to Saint Louis were crowded with spectators. The race started at New Orleans at five o'clock in the afternoon of June 30, 1870, and ended on July 4th, at Saint Louis. The winner was the *Robert E. Lee,* having run the upriver course in three days, eighteen hours, and fourteen minutes. After that event, the two vessels were the most renowned in the West and were looked on with awe by Midwesterners.

The next big town is Quincy, on the Illinois side of the river. In Mark Twain's days as a pilot, there were no bridges over the great river. But with the coming of the railroad the traffic axis of midland America became an east-west axis. And as railroad development first took place in the North, and as the east-west stream of traffic swelled rapidly in the expanding years after the Civil War, it followed that bridges were built with greater frequency in the North than in

THE *Natchez*

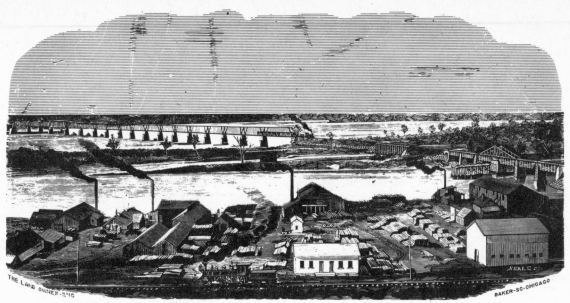

HANNIBAL AND SAINT JOSEPH RAILROAD BRIDGE, QUINCY

the South. The Hannibal and Saint Joseph Railroad Bridge at Quincy, Illinois, is one of the earliest of the transcontinental railroad spans over the river.

Above Quincy is the lively city of Keokuk, clinging to the slope of a green Iowa bluff. Just north of Keokuk, on the rolling Illinois side of the river, is one of the Midwest's most historic and romantic towns, Nauvoo. Here, in 1839, the founder of the Mormon Church, Joseph Smith, established headquarters for his sect, building a stately temple that could be seen a great distance up and down the Mississippi. And from here, too, after the murder in 1844 of Joseph Smith by a mob of non-Mormon settlers, Brigham Young led

FLOOD AT CAIRO

the exodus to Utah. On the Iowa side of the river lies Burlington which boomed rapidly, after it became the eastern terminus of the Burlington and Missouri Railroad.

Although mostly placid and of an orderly disposition, the Father of Waters sometimes goes on a rampage, as any normal human father may sometimes do, and when this happens there is vast destruction of property and often considerable loss of life. Because of its location at "The Meeting of the Waters," the old Illinois city of Cairo was often flooded in early times. One of the worst floods, which nearly destroyed Cairo, occurred on June 12, 1858. On that day, both the Mississippi and the Ohio, already high, quickly went over their banks. Settlers in the clearings and citizens in river towns fled in terror, seeking higher land. At about noon a crevasse opened in the Mississippi levee at Cairo. In almost an instant the streets of the town were flooded, with the water rising higher each minute. Above the cries of terror-stricken men, women, and children could be heard the angry roar of the floodwaters. Some families sought safety on makeshift rafts, on parts of collapsed houses and buildings. Soon the floodwaters had reached the embankment on the Ohio River side of the town, completely destroying a fine hotel and the tracks and equipment of the new Illinois

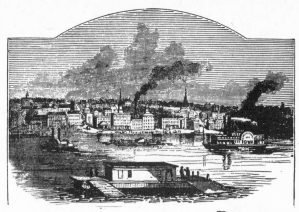

DAVENPORT

FORT ARMSTRONG

BURLINGTON

STORMING OF HOTEL AT BELLEVUE

GALENA

Central Railroad. The town was entirely under water and thus it remained for some days.

Many miles above Cairo are "The Quad Cities," in what was anciently known as "The Black Hawk Country." The Quad Cities are four independent towns all clustered together on the river: Rock Island, Moline and East Moline on the Illinois side, and Davenport on the Iowa side. Here was the bridge of the Rock Island Railroad, the one that was involved in a lawsuit in which the railroad was represented by Abraham Lincoln.

At Moline was the first factory built by John Deere for the manufacture of his steel plows, the same plows that made possible the vast corn and wheat belts of the Midwest; here, too, is the great Rock Island Arsenal. Of the many islands, large and small, in the Mississippi, Rock Island is the best known. The Rock Island Arsenal, with its limestone buildings, was established here by the government during the Civil War. It stands on the site of Fort Armstrong, which used to serve to protect the settlers of the Upper Mississippi Valley when Chief Black Hawk went on the warpath in 1832. Afterwards, Dred Scott was the servant of an officer at the garrison on the island.

North of Clinton lies a grand stretch of scenery, high, rugged palisades, higher even than those along the Hudson. They extend for miles on the Illinois side of the river. If it be sunset, these rocky cliffs will be painted bright orange, giving an impression long to be remembered. A few miles farther north is the Iowa river town of Bellevue. The early settlers of Bellevue, and of the Midwest in general, took the law into their own hands when the lawless among them got out of control.

It seems that during pioneer days a gang of outlaws, led by one William Brown, had established their headquarters by force in Bellevue's only hotel. As the gang was terrorizing the country for miles around, stealing horses, robbing lonely "movers" on their way westward, counterfeiting money, raiding farms, and engaging in piratical sorties on Mississippi flatboats and early steamboats, the law-abiding settlers of Bellevue decided that something drastic would have to be done. They held a meeting and planned a course of action. Not long afterward the outlaws were surprised to find their hotel surrounded by armed citizens. When the highwaymen refused to leave the hotel, the citizens opened fire. Rifle shots cracked thick and fast. Then the citizens rushed the hotel. After a few more shots the battle was over. When the smoke drifted away over the river, it was found that several had been killed on both sides. This battle ended once and for all the depredations of the William Brown gang.

On the Galena River, which comes down through the northwestern corner of Illinois, just a few miles inland, stands the thriving town of Galena, whose many fine plantation-style houses, on hillside terraces, testify to the one-time presence of wealthy Southern families. During the 1840s this town was of greater wealth and importance than Chicago, because of the lead mines in its vicinity. When the first railroad in Chicago was projected from that city to Galena, it was not called "The Chicago and Galena Union Railway," but "The Galena and Chicago Union Railway." Ulysses S. Grant worked as a clerk in a leather-goods store in Galena. Not far from the mouth of the Galena River there has always been a smoky haze on the Iowa side of the Father of Waters. This rises from Dubuque, where manufacturing was done even in the old days, when shot was made there.

Here the river begins to widen. Long slivers of islands appear. The rolling pastures of Wisconsin come into view. There are distant bluffs up ahead, on both sides of the river. Just after passing the wide mouth of the historic Wisconsin River, out of which

STEAM ICEBOAT

Father Marquette and Louis Jolliet paddled to discover the Upper Mississippi in 1673, lies Prairie du Chien, second oldest town in Wisconsin, one that began as a French trading post. The winters here are long and severe and the Mississippi is frozen solid. But ice on the river could not daunt Norman Wiard, an enterprising Prairie du Chien inventor, who in the winter of 1858 came up with his "steam ice boat." This was a conveyance making use of all the newest methods in steamboat architecture, including much ornamentation, only instead of being a big boat it was a big sled. Propelled by steam power, this iceboat was intended for winter passenger service between Prairie du Chien and Saint Paul. Although nothing more was heard of the "steam ice boat" after the winter of '58, it was nevertheless one more demonstration of the ever-alert inventive genius of Midwesterners seeking to master their environment.

North of La Crosse, another old Wisconsin town, and the Wisconsin coulee country, are the Minnesota bluffs. The Mississippi grows ever wider. The most beautiful

SAINT PAUL

LAKE PEPIN

MINNEHAHA FALLS

and impressive sight anywhere along the great river is Lake Pepin, a long body of water formed by the expansion of the Mississippi in this section. On the right, far off in the afternoon haze, stretch the bluffs, palisades, and rolling green hills of the Wisconsin shore, punctuated by the sharp eminence of Maiden Rock. On the other side, boldly against a declining summer sun, are more steep bluffs and rolling hills, those of the Minnesota shore. William Cullen Bryant wrote of this region: "This place ought to be visited by every poet and every painter in America. . . . It is a grief that Americans should wander off to the Rhine and the Danube, when in the Mississippi they have countless Rhines and Danubes. . . . Is Drachenfels one whit more castellated than any of the nameless bluffs about and around Trempealeau? All that is beautiful in lake-scenery, in lower mountain-scenery and river-scenery, is garnered here."

After some hours, riverboat travelers of yore would come to the mouth of the Saint Croix River, down which lumberjacks started their great log drives each spring,

[23]

THE MISSISSIPPI NEAR ITS SOURCE

FATHER HENNEPIN

INDIAN MISSION

guiding the timbers to sawmills in Minnesota and to Wisconsin towns along the Mississippi. At this point, the Father of Waters turns sharply northwestward, and some miles above this reach is Saint Paul.

Not least of the sights of Saint Paul and Minneapolis, the Twin Cities, are the historic Falls of Saint Anthony and the famous Minnehaha Falls, celebrated by Henry W. Longfellow in *The Song of Hiawatha*. It seems that the good but unreliable Father Hennepin, the early French explorer, never got beyond the Falls of Saint Anthony when he claimed to have reached the headwaters of the Mississippi in 1678. "Hennepin," says the historian Lossing, "was a man much given to romancing. . . . He claimed to have discovered the source of the Mississippi, when it is known that he never went above the Falls of Saint Anthony." It was power furnished by the harnessing of the Falls of Saint Anthony that made possible the operation of numerous sawmills here in the early days and, later, flour mills. Here the wheat of the North was, and still is, made into flour and shipped down the Mississippi in steamboats, to furnish bread to the Midwest.

Farther up the Mississippi, in the remote Indian country, were the very outposts of Midwestern civilization, the Indian missions. In such a mission, if the inland voyager arrived on a Sunday, he might hear, from a log church among the pines, the voice of a white preacher delivering the Word of God to bronzed natives of the Government Reservation. And on a weekday, he might listen to the voices of Indian children learning their lessons in a log schoolhouse presided over by the preacher's wife.

If he had ventured in his canoe still farther north on the Mississippi, up into the northwestern section of Minnesota, where the days are clear and bracing and the nights are a-glow with the Northern Lights, he would have arrived finally at the source of America's greatest river. This is Lake Itasca. Discovered in 1832 by the Government Indian Agent Henry R. Schoolcraft, this lake is located more than twenty-five hundred miles from the mouth of the Mississippi. It is the birthplace of the Father of Waters.

MIDLAND METROPOLIS

WHEN, during the American Revolution, a contingent of British soldiers arrived at the future site of Chicago, they found a lonely log cabin there occupied by a mulatto fur trader named Baptiste Point de Saible. He was Chicago's first recorded settler. He lived at the mouth of the Chicago River, trading with the Indians, shipping pelts to market, and welcoming an occasional *voyageur* from the French settlements to the north.

He first comes into the pages of history through this notation: "Baptiste Point de Saible, a handsome negro, well educated and settled at Eschikagou; but much in the French interest." These words were written on July 4, 1779. The writer of the notation was Colonel Arent Schuyler De Peyster, the then British commander at Michilimackinac, now Mackinac Island. That was at a time when the British had control of the wilderness country bordering the Great Lakes. Although identified in the notation as a Negro, Baptiste Point de Saible was the son of an educated French father and, presumably, of a Negro-slave mother. He is believed to have been born in Santo Domingo.

Although he did not seem to do much toward laying the foundation of this "youngest of the world's great cities," he appears to have occupied himself as an occasional fur trader. After seventeen years of frying his own bacon and listening to wintry lake winds howling around his eaves, Point de Saible sold his lone cabin to another trader and went to Peoria. The purchaser of the cabin was a Frenchman named Jean La Lime. La Lime continued the solitary life followed earlier by de Saible, although

Indians came once in a while and pitched their wigwams on the near-by prairies. By this time, however, the mouth of the Chicago River, which then curved just before it emptied into the lake, was becoming important as the gateway to the Chicago Portage, the link in the water route from the Great Lakes to the Mississippi River.

La Lime occupied the log dwelling until 1804, when it was purchased by John Kinzie, called "The Father of Chicago." In that year, too, there was completed, just across the river from the Kinzie cabin, a stockade called "Fort Dearborn." The builder of this fort was Captain John Whistler, an Irish-born officer of the American Army and grandfather of James A. McNeill Whistler. After becoming settled in his newly purchased cabin, John Kinzie, with the aid of his wife, got rid of its greasy odor, cleaned it up, and improved and enlarged it to such an extent that it became a "residence" and found its way into the history of Chicago as the city's first actual house.

Here John Kinzie quietly lived and traded and near by quietly lived and drilled the soldiers of Fort Dearborn, until the opening of the War of 1812. On the morning of August 15, 1812, the entire population of the settlement was suddenly attacked by overwhelming numbers of Indians in the sand hills about two miles south of Fort Dearborn. A short but fierce battle followed and when the yells of the Indians, the screams of women and children, and the sound of tomahawks and rifles subsided, it was found that twenty-six regulars, twelve militiamen, two women, and twelve children had been killed, as well as about two dozen Indians. After many of the surviving whites were taken prisoner, including John Kinzie, the maddened Indians set fire to Fort Dearborn and burned it to the ground. Thus ended the Fort Dearborn Massacre, or, as it is now known, "The Battle of Chi-

SITE OF CHICAGO IN 1779

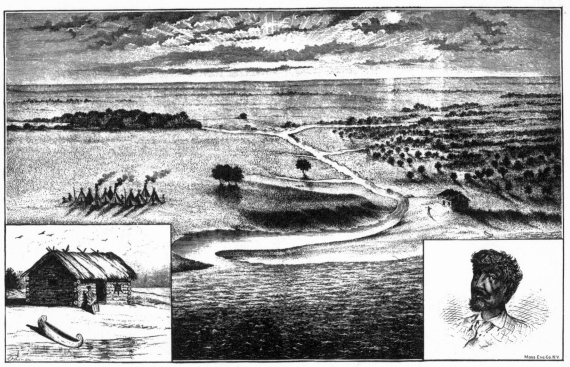

[27]

THE FIRST HOUSE IN CHICAGO

FORT DEARBORN IN 1830

cago." In the months following, weeds grew up in the deserted settlement of Chicago and an occasional crow sat on the charred ruins of Fort Dearborn. But in 1816 the fort was rebuilt, a new company of soldiers was garrisoned there, and John Kinzie and a

few other traders returned. The second Fort Dearborn remained in use until the Black Hawk War of 1832.

After 1832, the little log settlement of Chicago began to show signs of development. A canal was proposed, beginning at

THE CHICAGO RIVER IN PIONEER DAYS

WILLIAM B. OGDEN

THE SALOON BUILDING

Chicago and connecting the Great Lakes with the Mississippi River. This created a land boom. Soon the frontier town was full of speculators. Then the government made a harbor at the mouth of the Chicago River. This brought sailing vessels, lumber schooners. By now the population had increased to such an extent that on the 4th of March, 1837, the Legislature of Illinois approved the charter that made Chicago a city. As part of the general westward movement, especially after the building of the Erie Canal, more and more Easterners arrived in the infant city by the lake. Then came the bursting of the land-speculation balloon. A panic followed. But Chicago came out of this crisis in due time. She was not to be held back.

This determination to move forward, to expand, on the part of early Chicago was due in large measure to the leadership of the city's first mayor, William B. Ogden. He later became the builder of Chicago's first railroad, the Galena and Chicago Union (parent road of the present Chicago and North Western System), and achieved renown as one of America's foremost railroad magnates of the nineteenth century. In the beginning, Mayor Ogden demonstrated his resourcefulness when, with the approval

DEARBORN STREET BRIDGE

FRINK, WALKER AND COMPANY'S OFFICE

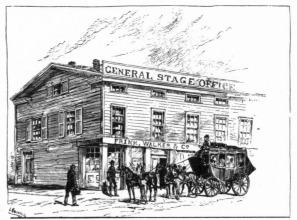

SAUGANASH HOTEL

of the Common Council, he set up a temporary "City Hall" in the Saloon Building,
which stood at the southeast corner of Lake
and Clark Streets. "At that time," says the
pioneer Chicago historian A. T. Andreas,
"it [the Saloon Building] was not only the
finest hall in Chicago, but was not eclipsed
by anything of the kind in the West. . . . The
name of this hall would, to the casual
reader, appear to connect it with a house of
no very good repute; but such an impression would be erroneous. The word 'saloon'
as applied to this edifice had a very differ-
ent meaning from what it now has. Its use
was synonymous with the French *salon,*
which means literally a grand and spacious
hall." This building served as a city hall
until 1841. At a later date, while in use as a
courtroom, the Saloon Building sheltered
Abraham Lincoln, who appeared there as a
trial lawyer. Meanwhile, Chicago had an
administrative building of its own, but this
soon proved inadequate to the growing city
and in 1851 work was started on a second
city hall (then called "court house"). This
served the city until it was destroyed in the
Great Fire of 1871. It was in the rotunda of
this second city hall that, on a sorrowful day

in 1865, thousands of Chicagoans viewed
the remains of the assassinated President
Lincoln.

It would appear, however, that in the
early days Chicago people were not always
satisfied with temporary arrangements. Consider, for example, the city's first draw-
bridge at Dearborn Street. It "was built in
1834 by a shipwright named Nelson R. Nor-
ton," says Andreas. A makeshift structure,
this bridge from the beginning "received
the blows of passing vessels and the curses
of pedestrians and drivers. . . . The Common Council ordered its removal in July,
1839. Many citizens were so afraid that the
Council would rescind this action, that a
large crowd gathered upon the river before
daylight, the next morning, and going to
work with a will, in a very short time
chopped the bridge to pieces."

A few blocks away from this ill-fated
bridge, at the southwest corner of Lake
and Dearborn Streets, stood Chicago's first
stagecoach office, Frink, Walker and Company. Here many stagecoaches arrived, and
departed, each day. As they bounced along
over plank roads, these stages would scatter
mud far and wide and call forth the wrath

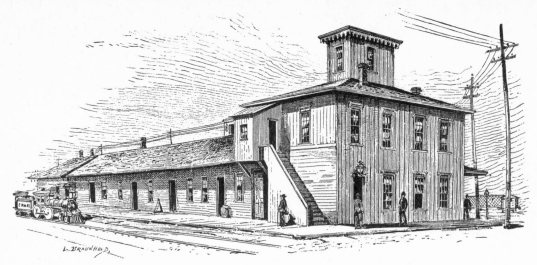

OLD GALENA DEPOT

of passing horsemen. Not a few passengers of the Frink, Walker stages, on arriving in the raw young city by the lake, would stop at Chicago's pioneer hotel, the Sauganash. This hotel was conducted by one of the most colorful and picturesque of early Chicago characters, Mark Beaubien. A traditionally jovial innkeeper and a fiddler of no mean ability, Mark Beaubien made his establishment a center of good cheer and merriment during the rough days of Chicago's infancy. His inn stood in the vicinity of Wolf Point, where the main channel of the Chicago River separates into two branches. On that same site, which now is the southeast corner of Lake Street and Wacker Drive, was built in after years the Wigwam, a convention hall in which Lincoln was nominated for the presidency.

The year 1848 marked a turning point in Chicago's history. Says Bessie Louise Pierce in *A History of Chicago*: "The coming of the railway symbolized the departure of the primitive structure of the old domestic economy and insured the manifest destiny of Chicago. On October 25, 1848, the Galena and Chicago Union Railroad sent out a locomotive with a tender and two cars,

which made its first run, a distance of five miles. In 1848, also, the electric telegraph provided Chicago a quick means of communication with the world outside. The era of beginnings was drawing to a close and the era of expansion was at hand."

Wrapped in greatcoats, holding on to their white beaver hats, smoke from the wood-burning locomotive blowing in their eyes, some one hundred leading citizens of Chicago, including the railway's president, William B. Ogden, sat on benches in the two open "cars" as the Galena and Chicago Union made its first run on that raw October day. Pulling the "cars" at a speed of between ten and fifteen miles an hour was "The Pioneer," a second-hand locomotive purchased by Ogden and his group in the East after attempts to buy a new one had failed. When the practicability of this first railroad was demonstrated, when the early objections to it by the merchants and Common Council of Chicago were overcome, the railroad built a wooden station with a cupola on it and from this cupola the road's superintendent, John B. Turner, scanned the Western prairie horizon with a spyglass, on the lookout for incoming trains.

McVICKER'S THEATRE

This original Galena Depot stood just west of Wolf Point, or near the present intersection of Canal and Kinzie Streets.

If railroad transportation had now come to the young frontier city of Chicago, it did not, however, immediately supplant that other mode of conveyance vital to the needs of the pioneer city: water transportation. Even after newer railroads than the Galena and Chicago Union had appeared, Chicago continued to be served by lake, river, and canal vessels. Not only was the narrow Chicago River crowded with barges of the Illinois and Michigan Canal and with energetic little tugboats, but it was frequently filled almost to capacity with big lumber schooners, loaded down with timber from the North Woods, and with gay white sidewheelers, their decks crowded with passengers from Buffalo and other Great Lakes cities. But in time the railroads outdistanced the steamship lines in the transportation race and Chicago was soon on its way toward becoming the railroad capital of the world.

At first full of backwoodsmen, traders, land speculators, farmers, river and lake roustabouts, and adventurers, almost all of whom chewed tobacco, drank whisky, and smoked cheroots, or stogies, Chicago, now that it was a growing railroad center, began

to acquire some of the refinements of Eastern cities. As more and more Yankees who had settled there made money, they demanded fine homes, carriages, schools, churches, theaters, and lyceum halls. A fashionable gathering place of those early days was McVicker's Theatre, which stood on the same site as the present large movie house of the same name. It was built in 1857 by James H. McVicker. On the open-

THE COFFEE HOUR

ing night, two performances were given, "The Honeymoon" and "Rough Diamond," and in both James McVicker "sustained the comedy element." His little daughter, Mary, who later starred there as Little Eva in "Uncle Tom's Cabin," afterward became the wife of the great American actor Edwin Booth. We may be sure that before and after attending a performance at McVicker's Theatre, many of the crinolined ladies of ante-bellum Chicago met in each other's residences on Michigan or Wabash Avenues for "The Coffee Hour," usually an occasion for social chat or an exchange of views on the acting of Edwin Booth, Joseph Jefferson, and other Thespians of the day, or a discussion of the newest display of diamonds at the jewelry shop of Mr. C. D. Peacock, then the leading gem merchant of the town.

As an indication of how quickly Chicago forged ahead as a railroad center, there was built, in 1857, a large stone edifice called the Great Central Railway Station. Located on the lake front, near the mouth of the river, this station served as a terminal not only for the new Illinois Central Railroad but for several other steam lines as well. One who often entered or left this station was Abraham Lincoln, who even then was being talked of as a presidential candidate. This terminal continued in use for many years and was among the few downtown Chicago buildings to escape destruction in the fire of 1871. It survives to the present time and is now used by the Illinois Central Railroad as a freight house. Another downtown structure to escape destruction in the fire was the town water reservoir. Before the fire it contained Chi-

GREAT CENTRAL RAILWAY STATION

cago's water supply, pumped from the lake; after the conflagration it served as temporary quarters for the Chicago Public Library, there having been built around it a temporary city hall, which came to be known as "The Rookery." Standing on the site of this reservoir today (southeast corner Adams and La Salle Streets) is an old-fashioned office building known as "The Rookery."

A Chicago event was one of the principal causes of the Civil War. That event was the nomination to the presidency of Abraham Lincoln, which occurred in the Wigwam, a frame hall built especially for the Republican National Convention, and which stood at the southeast corner of Wacker Drive and Lake Street. When, after the third ballot, with Lincoln needing only three or four more votes to be nominated, Carter of Ohio arose in the convention hall and stated: "I rise, Mr. Chairman, to announce the change of four votes of Ohio from Mr. Chase to Mr. Lincoln," there was a moment of dramatic silence and then, like the roar of a great tornado, came the jubilant yells and shrieks of thousands of visitors and delegates. Cannon boomed from the roof of the Wigwam, hats and handkerchiefs were tossed into the air, flags were waved, and processions formed in the streets of Chicago. One of their own kind, a backwoodsman of the Midwest, a country lawyer of the Prairie State, had been nominated for the office of President of the United States!

Soon the streets of Chicago were re-echoing to the martial steps of the men in blue as, with rifles over their shoulders, they marched off to battle fronts in the South. When they returned to Chicago in 1865,

CHICAGO RESERVOIR

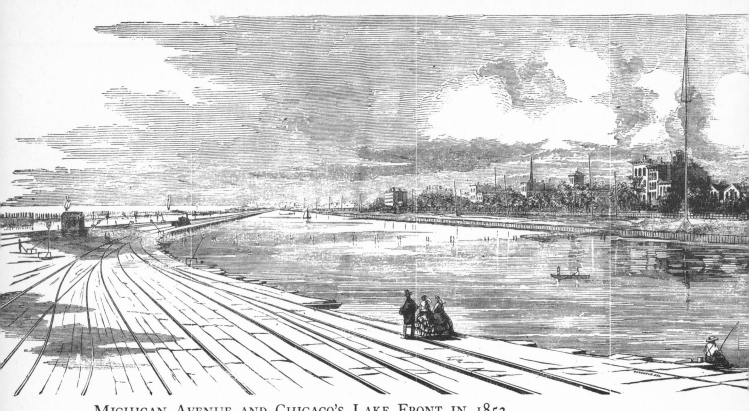

MICHIGAN AVENUE AND CHICAGO'S LAKE FRONT IN 1853

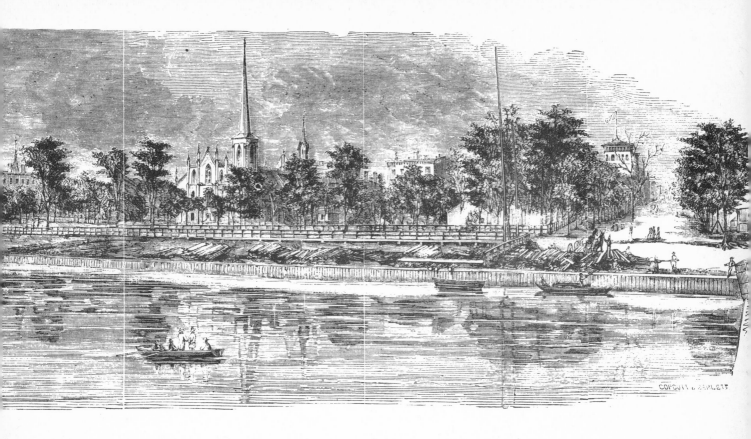

DOWNTOWN VIEW OF CHICAGO IN 1853

THE WIGWAM

INTERIOR OF WIGWAM

they found a bigger, livelier, and grander city than before the war. They saw more "steam cars" than previously. Railroad lines radiated in all directions from the town. Now Chicago had a much bigger railroad terminal than the original Great Central Railway Station on the lake front. This was the Michigan Southern and Rock Island Depot, the gateway to East and West. Its high arched roof, dimmed in a fog of smoke from funnel-shaped locomo-

tive stacks, resounded with the clamor of bells, hissing steam, bumping "cars," and shouting baggagemen. Where this "depot" stood on La Salle Street is now located the vast La Salle Street Station.

Now, too, Chicago boasted the elegant services of its "Pullman Hotel Car," the creation of a Chicago inventor, George M. Pullman. Such a car was ready for the much-advertised "Frank Leslie Excursion to the Pacific," sponsored by *Frank Leslie's*

MICHIGAN SOUTHERN AND ROCK ISLAND DEPOT

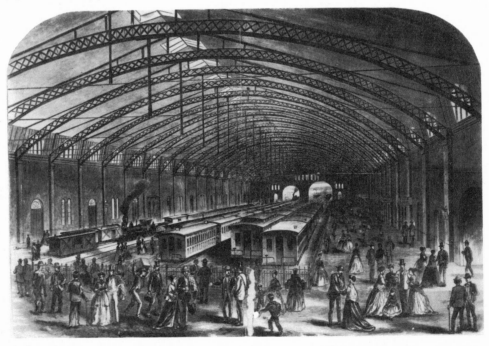

PULLMAN WASHROOM

PULLMAN PALACE CAR

Illustrated News shortly after the completion of the first transcontinental railroad. The guests on this excursion were quite thrilled at being able to dine while riding at twenty miles an hour in a Pullman Hotel Car. As to the dining facilities, one excursionist wrote: "Breakfast comes in by dainty courses; fish, fresh caught at the last station on our way, beefsteak and *champignons,* hot-rolls and corn-bread, and broiled chicken on toast, and potatoes stewed in cream or fried Saratoga fashion, with the best of coffee and tea, or a glass of milk, half-cream." If this be merely a breakfast layout, no wonder so many of our good fathers were afflicted with gout! Not only was the Pullman Hotel Car a dining car, but it was also a passenger coach, a sleeper, and a club car. Among the more important of its facilities were the washrooms. Morning ablutions were performed in zinc washstands with faucets operated by

FLEEING THE FLAMES OVER RANDOLPH STREET BRIDGE

MRS. O'LEARY'S COW

a hand pump. Very likely one's face needed a most thorough washing, for, despite the improvements and comforts of the Pullman Hotel Car, this was a day when railroad travel was still a matter of smoke, cinders, soot, and dust.

Traveling in their new Pullman Hotel Cars, riding about the streets in elegant victorias, living in stately mansions with mansard roofs, entertaining in gas-lit parlors, or on spacious piazzas, and making fortunes in wheat, hogs, cattle, lumber, and railroads, leading Chicagoans at the beginning of the 1870s were totally unprepared for what happened on a windy Sunday night in October of 1871. That night marked the beginning of the biggest and most disastrous event in Chicago's history, the Great Fire. It destroyed practically all of the downtown district and the city's North Side residential section and caused a loss of 250 lives and property damage amounting to more than two hundred million dollars. Although the exact cause of the conflagration

[38]

has never been officially determined, the legend persists that it was Mrs. O'Leary's cow who started it all by kicking over a kerosene lamp.

The fire spread rapidly and was soon out of control. It headed northeastward toward the downtown district, but in advance of it fled thousands of panic-stricken families, rushing headlong over the Randolph Street Bridge and other wooden bridges over the Chicago River. The roaring, searing flames swept through the downtown district, lighting up the night sky to a great height. Above the terrible sounds could be heard the tolling of the fire bell in the courthouse cupola and this tolling continued until the courthouse itself was devoured by the raging flames. Still the holocaust went on. Now it was destroying the magnificent Tremont House, finest hostelry of the day. After

crossing the main channel of the river, the great conflagration burned itself out on the morning of the third day, at a point near Lincoln Park.

THE POST OFFICE CAT

FIRE ATTACKS THE TREMONT HOUSE

With "The Wonder City of the West" now a mass of debris and smoking ruins, searching parties began work and, among other things, soon found that the post-office cat had saved her own life. She was discovered in a pail of water under the wreckage of the post-office building, apparently having overcome her strong objections to water long enough to withstand the heat of fire. Mr. William D. Kerfoot was the first person to build a temporary shack in the downtown district and resume business. Over the door of this shack he inscribed a legend, now famous in Chicago history, which read: ALL GONE BUT WIFE, CHILDREN AND ENERGY. It was not only Kerfoot's energy but the energy of all Chicagoans that, almost immediately after the Great Fire, brought into being a new Chicago.

As the years passed the Elegant Eighties

KERFOOT'S SHACK

THE OMNIBUS AND THE HANSOM CAB

merged into the Nobby Nineties, with cable cars replacing horse cars, and the new "bell" skirts replacing the bustles and draperies of a few years before. Preparations were begun for staging Chicago's greatest show, one that, said its planners, would outstrip anything of the kind ever before held in the world. This was the World's Columbian Exposition of 1893. In anticipation of that gala event, someone who preferred to be anonymous wrote a handbook called *Chicago by Day and by Night: The Pleasure Seeker's Guide to the Paris of America*. After describing the glories of Chicago's hotels, theaters, and restaurants, and after giving some instructions on the use of hansom cabs, omnibuses, and other modes of public conveyance in

"The Paris of America," our anonymous author then warns us of the "perils and pitfalls" to be found in the Windy City, cautioning us especially against the "gambling hells" that were all over the downtown district. *Chicago by Day and by Night* also sternly warns us to beware of indulging in casual flirtations in restaurants, hotel lobbies, and other public places, adding the maxim: "Be good and you will be happy."

When the World's Columbian Exposition opened in 1893, visitors beheld a classical "White City" reflected in the blue waters of Lake Michigan that has never, most of our now white-haired fathers maintain, been equaled. One of the principal sights of that international exposition was the Fine Arts Palace, which still stands on

A GAMBLING DEN

DANGEROUS FEMALE

FINE ARTS PALACE

MACHINERY HALL

its original site in Jackson Park, although reconstructed of more solid material than when first built. It is now known as "The Museum of Science and Industry." Another outstanding object at the World's Fair was the big Ferris wheel, which towered above the gaudy and picturesque amusement section known as "The Midway." A periodical of the time said of it: "The inventor [G. W. G. Ferris] declares that the conception was largely a matter of pique. 'The architects of the country,' he said recently, 'were getting all the credit for the Exposition, and I determined that the engineering profession should be represented by something that would stand as a monument.' " This was the first time the world had ever seen a Ferris wheel. Still another sight at the World's Fair that attracted wide attention was Machinery Hall, whose classical portico and stately façade looked down on the waters of a wide lagoon dotted with gondolas. And not least among the marvels at the White City in Chicago, although not so much in public view as the buildings, was the charming and beauteous Mrs. Potter Palmer, regal and bedia-monded "social queen" of Chicago during the Nobby Nineties and president of the exposition's Board of Lady Managers.

At the time of the exposition the Windy City contained quite a few other "wonders." One of these was the then "highest building in the world," the Masonic Temple, which towered to an unprecedented height of twenty-two stories at the northeast corner of State and Randolph Streets. Later called "The Capitol Building," this structure, which was designed by Burnham and Root, was finally torn down and replaced by a

MRS. POTTER PALMER

THE ORIGINAL FERRIS WHEEL

MASONIC TEMPLE, CHICAGO

MARSHALL FIELD IN THE '90s

pany. This house, too, is still in business.

A block west on Madison Street was the imposing home of the *Chicago Tribune*. Occupying the southeast corner of Madison and Dearborn Streets, the *Chicago Tribune* was then edited and published by Joseph Medill, former Mayor of Chicago, a promoter of the World's Fair of 1893 and grandfather of the present *Chicago Tribune* owner, Colonel Robert R. McCormick.

State Street was not entirely composed of two-story business block, which is completely modern.

On State Street also was that renowned "Emporium of the West," Marshall Field and Company, its elegant floors displaying merchandise from all parts of the world. Today, housed in an even greater store built on the same site, Marshall Field and Company continues to maintain its position as one of America's foremost department stores. Across the street from Field's in the 1890s stood the city's oldest and most exclusive jewelry store, C. D. Peacock and Com-

C. D. PEACOCK AND COMPANY

GRAND PACIFIC HOTEL

"dry goods" establishments. At Monroe Street was a magnificent hotel, the Palmer House. Among the marvels of this hotel, built by "The Father of State Street," Potter Palmer, was a barber shop whose marble floor was inlaid with silver dollars. Another big and glamorous hotel of that period was the Grand Pacific, which stood on Jackson Boulevard, between Clark and La Salle Streets. Here were the celebrated annual game dinners: Roman feasts of veni-

PALMER HOUSE

Chicago Tribune BUILDING IN THE '90s

son, squirrel, duck, rabbit, pheasant, and other choice viands, given by the Grand Pacific's hospitable proprietor, John B. Drake.

The Potter Palmers, Cyrus H. McCormicks, John V. Farwells, Joseph T. Ryersons, Lambert Trees, and other "First Families" of Chicago lived on "The Near North Side" during the 1890s. On Pine Street stood the Chicago Avenue Water Tower, which survived the Great Fire of '71 and which Oscar Wilde, on his visit to Chicago, called "a castellated monstrosity,"

GRAND PACIFIC LOBBY

MAHLON D. OGDEN RESIDENCE

CHICAGO WATER TOWER

CATHEDRAL OF THE HOLY NAME

a remark that ruffled the pride of the town's citizens. Still standing, the Gothic water tower now forms the center of "Towertown," as the city's Near North Side artists' colony is called. Another landmark in the same vicinity (Chicago Avenue and North State Street) is the Cathedral of the Holy Name, seat of the large Catholic archdiocese of Chicago. This limestone edifice, with its tall spire whose bell rings out on Sunday mornings, is a house of worship for prominent Irish, German, and other Catholic families, as well as for Catholic families not so prominent. Just south of the cathedral stands still another well-known Chicago sight, the Newberry Library, repository of many rare books on the humanities. On the site of this library was located the handsome early residence of Mahlon D. Ogden, brother of the first Mayor of Chicago. Miraculously escaping the flames of 1871, the Mahlon Ogden residence re-

DEARBORN PARK

MICHIGAN AVENUE FROM EXPOSITION BUILDING

STUDEBAKER BUILDING

Building but here, also, the famous Theodore Thomas Orchestra gave concerts on summer nights. This musical organization was the forerunner of the present world-renowned Chicago Symphony Orchestra.

Farther south on Michigan Avenue, past the Leland, the Richelieu, and other fashionable hotels of the time, was the Studebaker Building, behind whose plate-glass windows stood gleaming victorias, landaus, fringed-topped buggies, rock-a-ways, and other types of carriages, all from the South Bend factory of the Studebaker Brothers. With the arrival of the Automobile Age, the Studebaker Building was converted into a "temple of the arts," its name changed to the Fine Arts Building, and its floors occupied by musicians, artists, booksellers, and antique dealers. But the Studebaker Building was somewhat overshadowed by the Auditorium. This great stone edifice was Chicago's pride of the 1890s. A combined opera house, hotel, and office building, the Auditorium was designed in part by Louis Sullivan, who was eventually to become one of America's foremost architects, hailed as the father of the "Modern" movement. One of Sullivan's young assistants in designing the Auditorium was Frank Lloyd Wright. Another showplace in this

THE AUDITORIUM

mained standing until replaced by the Newberry Library.

On the south side of the river lies the central business district. In earlier days, Michigan Avenue was alive with victorias, landaus, and other smart turnouts. At the southwest corner of Michigan and Randolph was Dearborn Park, where, on one occasion, Abraham Lincoln made a speech. A few blocks south, on the city's "Lake Front," is the Art Institute, a magnificent building erected on the site of a huge, rambling community hall known as the Exposition Building. Not only were bicycle races, tug-of-war matches, political conventions, and stock shows held in the Exposition

part of Chicago of interest to visitors is the Coliseum, a large convention hall. Three men, Theodore Roosevelt, William Howard Taft, and Warren G. Harding, were nominated to the presidency within its fortresslike walls.

On "The Rialto" along Randolph Street were several public places with a distinctively Germanic atmosphere. German immigrants did as much to build Chicago and the Midwest as the Irish, the Scandinavians, or any other national group. On one side of Randolph Street is Henrici's Restaurant, founded by the Henrici brothers, descendants of a long line of German restaurateurs and caterers, and on the other side of the street rises the slender facade of the Schiller Theater, once the home of Teutonic opera. Another example of design by Louis Sullivan, the Schiller Theater afterward was renamed the Garrick Theater and continues in use today as a movie house. Most of the German element in Chicago lived on the north side of the city. In that section there survives the Germania Club, in a fine building, and, across from it, that popular restaurant the Red Star Inn, famed for its Teutonic victuals. Another popular gathering place of this section was Wright's Grove, where the

THE COLISEUM

SCHILLER THEATER

GERMANIA CLUB

Turnverein, or gymnastic societies, held picnics on Sunday afternoons in summer, joyously mixing gymnastic events and concerts with beer and pretzels.

On the northwest corner of Randolph and Clark Streets, across from the City Hall, stands that best-known of Rialto hotels, the Sherman House. It occupied the oldest hotel site in Illinois, the first Sherman House having been built there in 1837 by Francis C. Sherman, who afterward became a mayor of Chicago. From the upper

[49]

Picnic at Wright's Grove

Sherman House   Clark Street

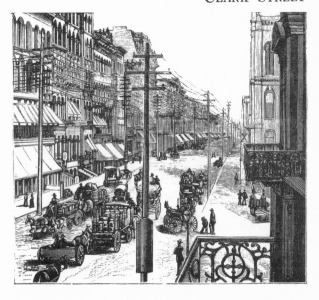

HOME INSURANCE BUILDING

CHICAGO BOARD OF TRADE

"THE PIT"

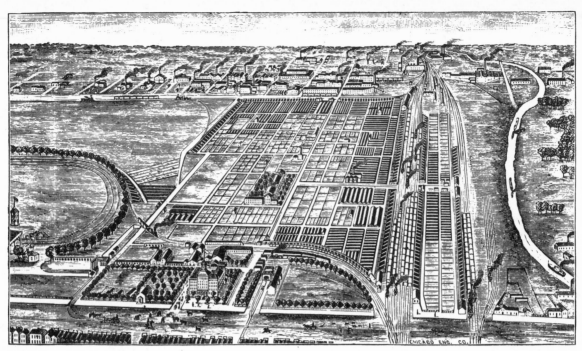

UNION STOCK YARDS

windows of an earlier Sherman House, there was a fine view of Clark Street just south of Randolph, noting among other things the wooden poles on each side of the street that supported a cobweb of light and power wires, which supplied the vital principle of that amazingly new form of illumination, the electric lamp.

In the Nobby Nineties La Salle Street was "The Wall Street of the West." Here one would see, at the northeast corner of La Salle and Adams Streets, a marvelous object—a tall office building erected on an all-steel framework, the Home Insurance Building, which was to become known as the world's first true skyscraper. At the foot of La Salle Street was an edifice surmounted by an imposing clock tower, the Board of Trade, one of the most important buildings in Chicago and the Midwest. Here was bought or sold, by brokers, all of the wheat and grain so plentifully supplied by the vast farms of the Midwest. This buy-

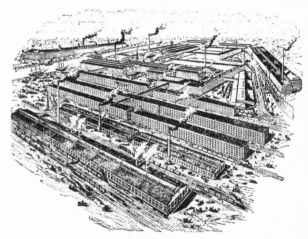

INTERNATIONAL HARVESTER COMPANY

ing and selling was done on the floor of "The Pit," which, with its shouting, pushing, hand-waving throng of men, resembled nothing so much as a madhouse. This building formed part of the background of *The Pit,* an exciting and realistic novel of the Wheat Empire by Frank Norris.

The industry that really put Chicago on

[52]

the map was meat packing. Presidents and princes, poets and peasants, came from all parts of the globe to view the mile-square Union Stock Yards on the city's Southwest Side, together with the adjoining slaughter-houses and processing plants of "Packing-town." The Union Stock Yards were built here in 1865 by John Sherman and a group of other leading citizens. It was Chicago's location in the heart of agricultural America that brought about its inevitable rise as the world's greatest meat-packing center. For the same reason, the Windy City leads all other cities of the globe in the manufacture of farm machinery. Not far from the Union Stock Yards is located the biggest of farm-machinery manufacturing plants, the International Harvester Company. Although the founder of this company, Cyrus Hall McCormick, invented his reaper in Virginia, he did not wait long before bringing it to Chicago, where in 1847 he built his first factory and shortly was sending out

reapers to the rapidly expanding Midwest.

Just as well known as Chicago's rail-roads, stockyards, manufacturing plants, and wheat pit are its cultural institutions: its universities, parks, museums, churches, and concert halls. Two of the city's oldest seats of higher learning, Northwestern University and the University of Chicago, are famed throughout the world for their contributions to knowledge. Still standing today on the Evanston campus of North-western University, which was founded in 1851 in a lawyer's office over a Chicago harness shop, is Old College, where, once each year, a candle symbolizing the light of education is lighted by the president and allowed to burn for fifteen minutes. At the same time, all over the world, similar candles are lighted by Northwestern alumni. Another old building still standing on the campus of Northwestern is University Hall, which was built in 1868. On the South Side of Chicago, constituting a veri-

NORTHWESTERN UNIVERSITY HALL

table "Gothic City," stands the University of Chicago. Although the present university is considered to have been founded in 1890, with a gift of $600,000 from John D. Rockefeller and an additional $400,000 from leading citizens of Chicago, this institution really had its beginning in the "Old" University of Chicago, a small Baptist college that, existing from 1857 to 1886, stood on a tract of land donated for the purpose by Senator Stephen A. Douglas. This tract was originally part of the Douglas estate, which then lay out in the country south of Chicago along the railroad Senator Douglas helped to establish, the Illinois Central. From this "Old" University of Chicago developed the present world-renowned institution on the Midway, an institution that attracts to its medieval halls thousands of young men and women from villages, towns, and cities in every part of the entire nation.

CITIES OF THE LAKES

THE COMPLETION of the Erie Canal in 1825 provided a great American artery of travel. This man-made waterway linking New York City with Buffalo played an important role in the settling of the Midwest. It led to the founding of villages and towns on the shorelines of the Great Lakes. And these villages and towns boomed into cities when "The Iron Horse" appeared.

The early Great Lakes villages and towns were destined to develop into important marketing, commercial, and industrial cities. Such energetic cities as Cleveland, Lorain, Sandusky, Toledo, Detroit, Bay City, Muskegon, Michigan City, Gary, Chicago, Kenosha, Racine, Milwaukee, and Duluth grew up rapidly. They compose the industrial belt of the Midwest, "The Workshop of America."

A hundred and fifty years ago Moses Cleaveland and a party of Connecticut Yankees landed on the south shore of Lake Erie, just west of the Pennsylvania border, on the site of the town of Conneaut. This was the beginning of the Western Reserve, a 120-mile strip of land in northern Ohio "reserved" by the State of Connecticut for its Revolutionary War veterans. When General Cleaveland and his group arrived at the mouth of Conneaut Creek on July 4, 1796, they found only a wide, lonely beach, but they staged a celebration not only in honor of the occasion but in honor of the independence of America.

The Cleaveland party did not long remain at Conneaut Creek, although only several years later other Yankees settled here and developed a shipping port. Heading westward through their Reserve, they fol-

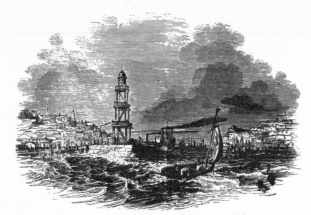

CLEVELAND HARBOR

CONNEAUT

ASHTABULA, OHIO, 1846

ASHTABULA IN 1887

lowed an old Indian trail along the level shore of Lake Erie. After traveling for some miles on the old trail, they arrived at the mouth of a good-sized river which the Indians called "The Ashtabula," meaning "The Place of Many Fish." General Cleaveland decided to call this river "Mary Esther" after his daughter back in Connecticut. When members of his party persisted in calling it "The Ashtabula," the good Connecticut general offered two casks of the grape to his followers if they would adopt the new name for the river. The story goes that they heartily agreed to this, as long as the wine lasted. Anyway, the name Ashtabula came back into use and in time was bestowed on a New England settlement here that rapidly grew into a fishing and shipping center. When the early Iowa artist-historian Henry Howe visited Ashtabula in the 1880s, he found it a thriving cosmopolitan city: "A new element has come into this region, emigrants from Finland; but recently subjects of the Czar. Down at Ashtabula Harbor is a large colony of Finns and Swedes, numbering several hundred. . . . They are highly thought of." Since then, Italian immigrants have settled in Ashtabula. Another settlement of Yankees was Geneva, the home of Platt R. Spencer, creator of the Spencerian penmanship system.

GENEVA

Few present-day towns of the old Western Reserve have preserved their New England atmosphere so well as Painesville, a quiet, leafy town of trim white homes with Georgian doorways, surrounded by picket fences. Just before the eastern outskirts of Cleveland is "Lawnfield," the home of President James A. Garfield at Mentor. In this rambling white house, with its many verandas, bays, dormers, and wing additions, Garfield staged the first "Front Porch" presidential campaign.

Two modes of transportation made Cleveland one of the Midwest's most important cities, the canal and the railroad. The Erie Canal, and, later, the Ohio and Erie Canal caused this early settlement of General Cleaveland's to boom rapidly into a bustling town. And after the railroads came, Cleveland expanded just as quickly into a city of almost the first magnitude. Cleveland also derived great impetus from its strategic position on the shore of Lake Erie.

Much of the rapid growth of Cleveland was also due to such industrial giants as John D. Rockefeller, Mark Hanna, and the Van Sweringens, and to such political leaders as Tom L. Johnson and Newton D. Baker. Today, in the midst of giant office buildings, there still stands the quaint old Weddell House, which was built more than

PLATT R. SPENCER

PAINESVILLE, OHIO, 1846

PAINESVILLE IN 1886

JAMES A. GARFIELD

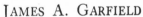

"LAWNFIELD"

THE CANAL AND THE RAILROAD

COURT HOUSE AT CLEVELAND

SUPERIOR AVENUE, CLEVELAND, IN 1846

a hundred years ago and which was early Cleveland's finest hotel. Here dusty and weary stagecoach and canal-boat travelers of pioneer times were given rest and refreshment. On his way to be inaugurated President in 1861, President-elect Lincoln stopped at the Weddell House and, from its second-floor balcony, delivered a brief address, saying: "If all do not join to save the good old ship of the Union this voyage, nobody will have a chance to pilot her on another."

In 1878 the forerunner of Cleveland's great High Level Bridge was built and became the wonder of its time, much traveled on by omnibuses, elegant victorias, fringed-topped buggies, and bicycles.

Cleveland's early citizens were an energetic, hard-working, and highly individualistic lot, and so, apparently, were its early editors. The editor who changed the spelling of the name of the city from "Cleaveland" to "Cleveland" did so because he did not have enough space on the masthead of his newly launched newspaper, *The Cleveland Gazette and Commercial Register.* Without consulting anyone, he simply left out the first "a" in Cleaveland. Then there was another editor, a woman. A periodical of the time, under the heading "Discomfiture of an Editress," tells us: "It appears that the city of Cleveland, Ohio, was blessed by the weekly production of a paper called *The Spy,* which contained some very 'spicy' articles, and, being edited by a female, made it its especial vocation to pry into other people's business. . . . In an evil hour, the editress animadverted in strong terms upon an employé of the Cleveland and Toledo Railway." The enraged railroader "invaded" the lady editor's "sanctum" and a fight followed, as the editress was a lady of considerable spirit. Fists were swung and ink bottles thrown. Continues the periodical: "The noise attracted the attention of the foreman of the compositors,

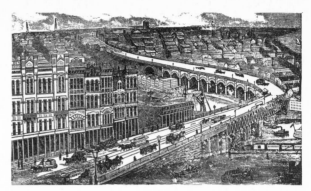

SUPERIOR AVENUE VIADUCT

ATTACK ON "LADY EDITOR"

LIGHTHOUSE, CLEVELAND

SLAB HALL

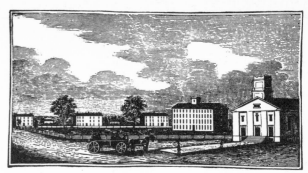

OBERLIN COLLEGE IN 1846

SANDUSKY HARBOR

BIRTHPLACE OF THOMAS A. EDISON

THOMAS A. EDISON

who came to the lady's relief, but was attacked with a hammer and put to flight, after which the railroader celebrated his triumph by smashing the furniture and the presses, and throwing the type out of the window, and then retired, covered with glory and ink. The lady was left *hors de combat* on the field, but recovered in time to issue the paper as usual."

Cleveland citizens of that time, when not working hard, sought pleasure in quiet ways. A favorite pastime then, especially on Sunday afternoons, was a leisurely ride or stroll on Cleveland's lake front in the vicinity of the lighthouse at the foot of Water Street. With the ladies attired in their best crinolines and bonnets and escorted by stovepipe-hatted gentlemen in skin-tight trousers, this lake-front promenade was a colorful sight. Not least among its delights was the fine view of Lake Erie, its placid blue expanse dotted with the white sails of lumber schooners or smudged here and there by the smoke of steamships.

Some twenty-five miles southwest of Cleveland stands Oberlin College, one of the oldest institutions of higher learning in the Midwest and the world's first coeducational college. It is also unique as the first such institution to admit Negroes. When first opened in 1833, Oberlin College consisted of but a single barrack-like building, in the northern Ohio woods, which in time came to be known as "Slab Hall."

West of Oberlin College is Sandusky. Even as far back as a hundred years ago, Sandusky was a bustling lake port.

Thomas A. Edison was born in Milan, a quiet little town some twelve miles south of Sandusky, in 1847, in a little red brick cottage. Another noted American associated with the Sandusky region was the financier Jay Cooke. Just north of Sandusky, on the wooded island of Gibraltar in Put-in-Bay, the man who financed the Civil War built an island castle in the late 1860s that became a showplace of the Great Lakes area.

This stone castle, with its fifteen rooms and octagonal tower, still stands on Gibraltar Island. Still standing on the island, too, is a monument erected by Jay Cooke in memory of the famous American naval commander Oliver Hazard Perry. Off Put-in-Bay Perry fought and won the only naval battle ever to occur in the Midwest, the Battle of Lake Erie, an important en-

JAY COOKE

GIBRALTAR ISLAND

MEMORIAL SERVICE, PUT-IN-BAY

"SPIEGEL GROVE"

counter in the War of 1812. After the battle Perry sent to General Harrison his famous message: "We have met the enemy and they are ours." In the years just before the Civil War, it was the custom in Sandusky to stage an annual celebration of Perry's victory, on South Bass Island, combining this with a memorial service under a great old willow tree which marked the graves of some of Perry's fallen seamen

Another historic house in the Sandusky region which still stands is the home of President Rutherford B. Hayes at Fremont, southwest some twenty miles from Sandusky. The beautiful estate in which the old red-brick Hayes mansion is situated is called "Spiegel Grove." Before this house was built in 1860 by President Hayes' uncle and boyhood guardian, Sardis Birchard, there was located here a charming grove of elms, oaks, and walnuts, which, reflected in several reedy pools of water, made a vivid impression on Sardis Birchard. So he called his estate "Spiegel Grove" after the German word *Spiegel,* which means "mirror."

TOLEDO HARBOR

To this parklike estate Rutherford B. Hayes retired following his term as President, an administration that began with the fireworks of the heated Hayes-Tilden Controversy.

The Battle of Fallen Timbers was perhaps one of the most decisive encounters in Midwestern annals. Fought on a hill overlooking the Maumee River, some ten miles southwest of Toledo, it occurred on August

BATTLE OF FALLEN TIMBERS

20, 1794, and brought undying fame to General "Mad Anthony" Wayne. By winning this battle, General Wayne and his soldiers removed for some years the menace of unexpected Indian attacks in the great wilderness region west of the Alleghenies, and this, in turn, made possible the safe settlement and eventual growth of "The Cities of the Lakes."

In a little less than two decades, however, the Indians were on the warpath again, this time aroused by the British in the War of 1812. With the Indian danger once more removed after the War of 1812 and with the coming of the Wabash and Erie Canal, Toledo grew rapidly as a lake-shipping port. In 1846 three million bushels of foodstuffs passed through its harbor.

Of greater interest than its position as a waterway terminal is the fact that it was from Toledo that the first railroad train of interior America started in 1836. This original railroad, forerunner of the vast network of roads which were later to populate and build the Midwest, was the Erie and Kalamazoo.

If Toledo gave the Midwest its first railroad train, Detroit gave it its first automobile, or at least an automobile of the type all could afford to buy. Detroit began as an

ERIE AND KALAMAZOO RAILROAD

early French trading post, having been established in 1701 by Antoine de la Mothe Cadillac, an agent of Louis XIV. Here Cadillac built a fort, which he named Fort Pontchartrain after France's then Minister of Marine. It was around this fort that French habitants and *voyageurs* settled and laid the foundations for what later became Detroit.

After the French and Indian War, Detroit came into the possession of the English, but was nearly lost to the latter when the famed Ottawa chief Pontiac tried to capture it by trickery in 1763. Pretending to seek peaceful council, Pontiac and some of his principal aides, with sawed-off muskets hidden under their blankets, were received by Major Gladwyn, commandant of the fort at Detroit. But Major Gladwyn, who had been warned of the plot by an

Indian girl, was ready. Just when Pontiac was about to present a gift belt to the major, this gesture having been agreed on by the Indians as a signal for their uprising, a sudden roll of drums at the door of the council house was heard, officers drew their swords and soldiers their muskets, and Pontiac and his aides were made prisoners. When this fact was made known to the Indians outside the fort, they scattered in all directions and thus came to an end the famous Pontiac Conspiracy.

During the War of 1812, however, Detroit fell once again into the hands of the British, though only for a brief time. It was in a battle fought to recapture the city from the British and their Indian allies that another celebrated chief, Tecumseh, was killed. He was at the head of an army of between twelve and fifteen hundred Indian warriors when the engagement opened. Opposing him at this point was the American commander Colonel Johnson of Kentucky.

Today in the downtown district of Detroit you will find a small, triangular-shaped spot called "Capitol Park." Here, for more than sixty-five years, stood Michigan's first capitol building. It was built in 1828, served as territorial and State capitol until 1847, and was destroyed by fire early in the 1890s. After being abandoned as a State capitol, this somewhat ornate struc-

PONTIAC'S CONSPIRACY

DEATH OF TECUMSEH

ture, with its Greek portico and un-Greek tower, served as a schoolhouse.

One of the oldest and best-known families of pioneer Detroit was the Campaus. An interesting sidelight on this family was the homes built in Detroit by each succeeding Campau generation, a series of dwelling houses that may be said to illustrate the development of domestic architecture in the central-states region. The first of these houses, that were erected by Jacques Campau about 1757, was a simple gabled structure built of vertical logs in the French style. Later backwoods settlers erected cabins of horizontal logs, a method introduced

into America by the Swedish colonists on the Delaware River. Near his home, about the year 1778, Jacques Campau built a small church.

In 1796, when the Stars and Stripes was first raised over Detroit, a son of Jacques Campau, Joseph, built the second of the family dwellings. Used as both a store and a home, the Joseph Campau abode was an architectural advance on the earlier house, with gambrel roof and dormers. In this house, which stood at No. 140 Jefferson Avenue, Joseph Campau lived until his death in 1863. On the Detroit River, at the rear of his home, he maintained a com-

OLD STATE HOUSE, DETROIT

JACQUES CAMPAU CABIN, c. 1757

THEODORE CAMPAU MANSION, 1869

JOSEPH CAMPAU RESIDENCE, 1796

modious warehouse and a dock for the accommodation of his *bateaux*.

With expanding family fortunes, as Detroit increased in population, there appeared the third Campau dwelling house. This was erected by Theodore J. Campau in 1869 and stood at 500 Jefferson Avenue. Like so many other Midwestern homes of wealth at that time, the Theodore Campau residence had all of the details of a Victorian mansion: ornamental cupola, tall bay windows, stone steps, and an inviting portico. At the rear of the mansion stood the coachhouse and stables, which housed the elegant Campau carriages and fine blooded

horses, an especial pride of the family.

Paralleling the Detroit River, and looking out on historic Belle Isle, Jefferson Avenue was the principal street of Detroit in the early days. And a central gathering place was Campus Martius, a plaza which previously had served as a military drill ground. Near it stood the old City Hall, built in 1835, and the original City Market, as well as two leading hotels of pioneer times, the Mansion House and the National. From Campus Martius evolved the present Cadillac Square, throbbing heart of downtown Detroit.

Where now stand the great long factories,

DETROIT IN THE 1850s

FERRY SEED FARM

with their rows of tall smokestacks, of the River Rouge Plant of the Ford Motor Company, there existed, half a century ago, the extensive seed farm of D. M. Ferry and Company. It embraced several hundred acres along Grand River Avenue.

Still standing today, only now much darkened with grime and soot, is Detroit's City Hall, a grandiose edifice designed in the French Renaissance style and completed in 1871. For some years after its completion a watchman was always on duty in the ornate central tower of the City Hall, stationed there to sound the alarm to the Volunteer Fire Department in case of a blaze anywhere in the city. The bell used for this purpose still hangs in the tower. On the façade of this building, which overlooked Campus Martius, are statues of Cadillac, Father Gabriel Richard, and other early Detroit historical personages, these having been presented to the city by

the late Bela Hubbard, pioneer surveyor and Michigan historian.

As is well known, the State of Michigan fifty or seventy-five years ago produced much, if not most, of the nation's lumber. Although the sturdy, red-shirted lumberjacks have long since gone from the state, they left behind them not only stumps and cut-over land but the giantesque figure of Paul Bunyan, who, along with Mike Fink and Johnny Appleseed, is one of the Midwest's best-known folk heroes. Made possible by the logger's ax, and still flourishing today in the same role, is Grand Rapids, which, at the turn of the century, produced more furniture than any other city in America. From Grand Rapids came the marble-topped tables, whatnots, walnut chests, horsehair rockers, plush sofas, and other articles of furniture that crowded the "front rooms" of Midwestern homes in days gone by.

Even if they were the tools of ruthless lumber barons, the loggers of early Michigan were a heroic race of men. In the frozen winter months, the big woods re-echoed to the clear ring of their axes or the rhythmic sound of their crosscut saws. One by one, with a shout of "Timber!" from the men, the great trees crashed to the ground with a thundering roar. Breathing steam from their nostrils, horses hauled the long logs on the tote road to the nearest river-bank. In the spring the ice in the rivers thawed, loosening the logs. Then began the great spring drives on the rivers, with thousands of logs moving downstream. It was up to the lumberjack, armed with his peavey, or pike-pole, his feet encased in calked boots, to prevent the logs from jamming. The lumberjack, as he skillfully rode a log on a drive, seemed more like a god than a man.

After the spring drive there came, during the summer months, the screech and scream of the sawmill as logs were fashioned into boards and planks. This finished lumber, in the holds of sailing vessels or on board freight trains, went to Grand Rapids, or to that dynamic capital of the interior country, Chicago. The timber that went to Chicago was shipped out to become homes and buildings throughout the nation.

The next city of importance in this area

CITY HALL, DETROIT, CIRCA 1871

LUMBERING

is Milwaukee, famous for its beer. Many years ago, Milwaukee was renowned for another type of creamy product, a superior quality of brick widely known as "Milwaukee Cream." Not a few stately mansions were admired in the old days because of their façades of Milwaukee Cream brick. Milwaukee was the inspiration of two songs which have since become Midwestern folk tunes: "Lost on the *Lady Elgin,*" commemorating a shipwreck on Lake Michigan, and "Burning of the Newhall House," commemorating a tragic Milwaukee hotel fire. Milwaukee still has much of its old-time German flavor, with cafes and beer gardens furnishing both *Sauerbraten-mit-*

Knoedeln and the fine music of Beethoven.

Supplier of iron ore to the blast furnaces of the Workshop of America is Duluth, located at the far-off head of Lake Superior. Founded as a French trading post by Daniel Greysolon, Sieur Du Lhut, this largest of northern Minnesota cities is a port of call for the long, low freighters that carry iron ore from the Mesabi and other ranges to the mills at Gary, Cleveland, and other industrial cities of the Great Lakes region. It is also the gateway to the vacation lands of the North Woods, through which Midwesterners and others escape from hot cities and towns to cool forests and silent lakes.

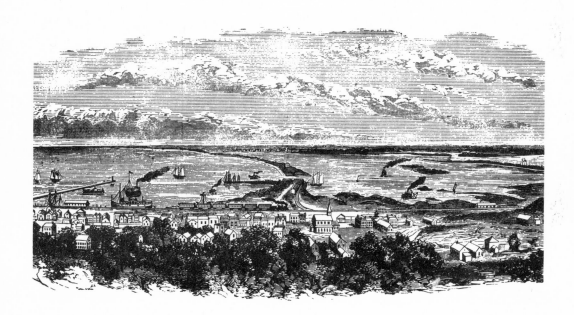

WHEATLANDS AND CORNFIELDS

IT WAS inland America's rich, level soil, stretching for several thousand miles from the Alleghenies to the Rockies, that brought peoples from all over the world to found a new civilization and create a free and democratic mode of life. In the beginning, Midwesterners were farmers. It was the grainlands of the Upper Mississippi Valley, those vast, magnificent gold-and-green acres, that created the first lasting wealth of the area and made possible the building of the towns and cities.

During the first half of the nineteenth century the Midwest was largely agricultural. After the Civil War, it developed quickly as an industrial region, without, however, losing its status as the grain-producing area of the nation.

What manner of people were they who laid the foundations of this huge mid-con-tinental region? By far the greater number of earliest Midwestern settlers were native Americans of English or Scotch-Irish origin and these folk set the general pattern of life in the region, being themselves only slightly affected by the ways of European immigrants. The Germans, the Irish, the French, the Swedes, the Dutch, and the Danes conformed by and large to this pattern, but they enriched it with fresh color, embroidering on it designs of their own which lent chromatic variety to the whole. In time, the fabric of Midwestern civilization mellowed, but it has never become exactly homogeneous in its broad outline.

The western settlers from the Carolinas, Virginia, Maryland, and the New England States felt that there was a land of bounty beyond the mountain ridges. It was a serious and disturbing fact that the lands they

PIONEER

JOURNEY INTO THE WILDERNESS

had cultivated had ceased to produce such great harvests of grain and tobacco as in the "olden time" of colonial government. Furthermore, the laws of primogeniture and entail had caused the younger sons of colonial farmers to think of bettering their fortunes in the rich new lands which they had heard lay out beyond the mountains. There were many scores of landless poor, among whom were the descendants of indentured servants and newcomers from England who had no wealth but their own physical strength.

The first families to make their way to the western country, those who followed Daniel Boone's blazed trails on horseback, or in covered wagons, surmounted what to the modern traveler would be insuperable difficulties. There were widespread swamps and marshes. In going through the vast dark forests, migrants did so at the risk of capture, or perhaps sudden death, at the hands of hostile Indians. Rest was had at night on the open prairies.

Usually, the head of the family walked over the trail beside his team, while his wife and children rode in a rough farm wagon laden with household utensils. Sometimes a child would become ill and then the family pitched camp and waited until the child grew healthy again, or died. A father would sometimes be forced to dig a grave in the lonely forest. One can imagine the desolation of such a family. But despite such tragedies, the family must soon be on the move again.

The first requisite of the settler was his gun. The next most important was his ax. And if he did not possess a tinderbox, he must carry fire with him in an iron pot with a perforated tin lid. It was the boast of many a pioneer Midwestern householder that the fire in his fireplace had come from Virginia or North Carolina. We are told that one Illinois family preserved their fire by careful banking and tending until the year 1840, having carried it from Virginia to Kentucky in the late eighteenth century and thence across the Ohio River into Illinois.

The first rude log huts built by the newcomers into the western wilds were so forbidding as to seem by later standards unlivable. Many of them had no windows, and instead of a door there was often only a curtain of deer hide. If there was a window it was usually covered with paper thickly coated with bear's grease, which admitted

BUILDING THE CABIN HOME

THE PIONEER AND HIS AX

oaken or hickory containers, and jugs and ewers of earthenware.

Game was usually plentiful, though in some exceptionally cold winters the deer, bear, and smaller animals were perverse enough to wander far away from the settled regions, so that the hunter often came home with no meat. Always provision had to be made in the summer and fall for a lean winter. Corn was shelled and laid by, hogs and venison were salted and stored in barrels, and a barrel of meal stood in a corner of the

PLOWING

SPINNING

a diluted light and was fairly waterproof. The floors were bare earth. Sometimes a semblance of comfort was achieved by a buffalo hide or deerskin rug before the fireplace.

All of the cooking was done in the fireplace. Cooking utensils were of the simplest. A Dutch oven or an iron kettle, and perhaps a skillet and a copper saucepan, comprised the usual assortment of vessels, though there were wooden lard buckets, water buckets, soap buckets, and other stout

HUNTERS AND TRAPPERS AT NIGHT

cabin. A few chickens might even be sheltered in the cabin.

When spring came to the western woods and fields, the pioneer family was so eager for a taste of green food that the women and children spent the first warm bright days gathering and preparing wild "sallet," or dandelion, wild lettuce, sourdock, and the young tender shoots of pokeweed, which were cooked in the big iron kettle.

As for the furnishings of an early Midwestern cabin, there was a slab-wood or puncheon table made of half-hewn logs, there were puncheon benches, and there was a built-in bedstead against the wall. This last was made, according to the best tradition, of sassafras wood, which was thought to discourage unwelcome insects.

It was a simple arrangement: two poles extended at right angles from the walls, supported by a stake driven into the earthen floor at the outer corner. Thongs or ropes were strung between the poles and a mattress was made of cornhusks, leaves, or feathers. Hides, perhaps a woolen blanket or two from the East, and whatever makeshift material could be procured were the rule for covering. Often the young ones slept on the floor on a bed of leaves.

When the clothing the pioneers brought with them had been worn to shreds, the women of the family wove linen cloth from their patches of home-grown flax. Sometimes this was very fine and beautiful, and often the finished cloth was bleached twenty or thirty times by hourly dampening in the

WASHING DAY

hot sun. More often it was grayish and streaked, and the coarsest variety, called towlinen, was used for men's summer work shirts and jeans. The jeans were frequently dyed brown in a strong infusion of butternut hulls. When the warp of the material was of linen and the weft of wool, it was called linsey-woolsey.

In the earliest days there were few sheep among the farmers, for the presence of so many wolves made their raising too hazardous. In winter, the men of the family wore buckskin suits and either leather boots or elongated moccasins that were cut so as to extend just above the knee. The buckskin jackets usually had a fringed cape, as well as fringed lower edge. They were designed

WOLF ATTACK

with a generous overlap in front, which added warmth to the garment and also furnished a repository for small game when the wearer was hunting. Children were dressed just as their parents, except that in summer small boys nearly always wore only towlinen shirts, without any breeches or underclothing.

Far more serious than the mere discomforts of life in the wild new land were the actual dangers that confronted the settler. Indian raids were frequent and often terrible; wild animals lurked in the underbrush: catamounts, bears, gray wolves, and one had always to fear the rattler, the copperhead, and the cottonmouth. And there was the frightful ague, then sometimes

HARVESTING

BORDER SETTLERS IN OHIO

PLANTING CORN

BACKWOODSMEN AT CAMP

called "The Illinois Shakes," or "chills and fever," which afflicted nearly everybody in certain localities. Worse than the ague was the "milk sick," a mysterious disease that broke out first among cattle and then attacked human beings. Even chickens were affected by this malady and it was almost always fatal.

Physicians of the time (and there were very few medical men in the western country during the early years) doctored mostly with herbs and simples, and some of the remedies they administered to their patients were odd in the extreme, even verging on the magical. Medical practice was almost entirely a matter of bloodletting and folklore.

Houseflies were at first unknown in the wilderness. It was only when organic refuse began to collect around the settlements that they made their appearance. But there were many mosquitoes, chiefly the relatively harmless *Culex,* but almost as widespread was the malaria-carrying *Anopheles*. The settlers, of course, did not associate malaria with mosquito bites. This scourge of pioneer life was generally considered as a virus that seeped into the hu-

man system through the nostrils from the miasma of swamps.

Establishing the first elements of a home, roof, fireside, and food was quickly followed by clearing and cultivation of the soil. In the necessary haste to plant corn the settlers could not wait to clear their fields in the painful and tedious manner they had learned in the Eastern states. As they migrated westward, they found ever new forests to cut down and uproot. And they found vast prairies of grass. It was thought at first that the prairie lands would never produce sufficient crops to make their cultivation worth while, for where only grass grew one could not expect that the soil was rich enough for grain. The grass would serve for grazing. This was the tall bluestem that could hide a herd of cattle and that undulated in the wind like the waves of a great green ocean. Only the leaf mold of the woodlands was considered suitable for plowing and sowing.

The clearing of the forests proceeded slowly. At first the settler girdled the trees on a few acres, leaving them to die; the following spring he planted his crops in rows among the dead trees and enough sunlight penetrated through the bare branches to waken the seeds into green life. Perhaps he had only a "hoe plow" with which he scratched the soil by hand, or an all-wooden horse plow, which often broke and splintered on roots and stones. In the years just before 1800 there came into use the Carey plow, which had a stout iron-sheathed blade that could cut through the most unyielding sod and was not greatly damaged by stony or woody obstructions.

who later made their homes beyond the Mississippi. In his last days, after civilization had caught up with him and he settled down with relatives in Missouri, Daniel Boone spent his time in making powder horns for his grandchildren, repairing rifles, and the daily polishing of a coffin that he had made for himself. It is said that this coffin was the second of two he had made. Since the first of the two coffins was not the right size for Boone, he gave

PIONEER SCHOOLHOUSE

ORIGINAL McCORMICK REAPER

The work of clearing was hard and tedious. Lumber was so little needed in the new land that an incalculable number of logs were piled up and burned. Within fairly recent years the stumps of enormous walnut trees, too large for the pioneers to uproot, and left by them on the ground, have yielded precious veneering material for cabinetmakers.

As the lower Midwest became more and more settled, hunters, trappers, and backwoodsmen of the type of Daniel Boone pushed farther and farther out onto the Western prairies, finding trails for those

it to his son-in-law, Flanders Callaway.

The New Englanders who came west in the early nineteenth century, while more aggressive in some ways than the Virginians and North Carolinians, were inexperienced in Indian warfare and woodcraft and were generally unused to such an intensely rugged way of life. Many of them had farm backgrounds, but it was the neat, orderly, well-established rural life of the much more closely settled Northeast that they had left behind them when they ventured westward. They learned quickly and about four years after the Chicago Massacre of 1812, now called the Battle of Chicago, they came pouring in by the hundreds to seek their fortunes in the rapidly expanding frontier region.

Almost from the first, the New Englanders displayed more commercial than agricultural interest in the newly developing Midwest. The majority of them established themselves in towns and villages and set up as storekeepers, manufacturers, and traders of all sorts. The great land boom of the third decade of the nineteenth century found numbers of them becoming rich overnight.

The New Englanders became the bone and sinew of the greatest farm-and-factory

MECHANICAL CORN PLANTER

DOG-POWER CHURN

WOOLMAN'S PATENT FARM GATE

civilization the world has known. They possessed inventive genius; they were unfailingly industrious; they were superb engineers; and above all, they brought with them to the West the quality of moral stamina that has been referred to in a very narrow sense as "New England conscience."

As the early years of the nineteenth century unfolded, more and more farms appeared where once were great dark stands of pine and vast acres of prairie grass. But this agricultural development was slow until there appeared the invention that made the Midwest what it is today. This was the reaping machine created by Cyrus Hall McCormick. Almost from the beginning farmers demanded the McCormick reaper. McCormick began to manufacture it in Chicago and brought to the infant city an industry that helped to boost that community into the status of capital of the Midwest.

In the rapidly expanding years after the Civil War, there was an increasing demand for labor-saving devices. The high cost of hired labor and the tedious, profitless "family" production of raw products and manufactured goods called for a new organization of agriculture and industry on a mechanized basis. There followed, year after year in rapid succession, a host of inventions, all intended to lighten the load of muscle-weary farmers in the agrarian Midwest. Inventors of the time vied with each

SORGHUM MILL

other in producing devices, gadgets, and machines for the benefit of tillers of the soil.

There was, for example, a mechanical corn planter. But if the farmer's burdens were lightened by mechanical devices in those early days, not so, apparently, were the dog's. A device for putting the faithful if lazy farm hound to work was the dog-power churn. And if the dog refused to earn his keep thus, the machine could be operated by "a docile sheep."

Woolman's Patent Farm Gate, we are told, was "so constructed as to be opened, closed and fastened without lighting from the carriage." If, so far as can be ascertained, Mr. Woolman's Patent Farm Gate cannot be had today, we certainly have no difficulty in obtaining at present that delicious "sweetinin'" sorghum. Mere mention of it brings a vision of a stack of wheatcakes oozing on all sides with sorghum, a cup of steaming coffee standing next to it. An efficient way in which our forefathers could have prepared this sirup was through the use of Power's Patent Sorghum Mill. The power for this mill was provided by a pair of horses driven by the farmer's wife, who sat on a revolving platform. Nothing is said about the possibility of the farmer's wife becoming dizzy as the platform turned around all day. A machine that threatened the extinction of that most enjoyable of old-time Midwestern frolics, the husking bee, was Spear's Patent Corn Husker, which

husked corn well and with great rapidity.

Some idea of how such great stacks of hay were piled up in Indiana and Illinois farmyards during hot midsummer days might be gained from a study of Porter's Patent Derrick and Champion Hay-Carrier. This derrick and hay carrier in no way lessened the joys of farm youngsters at hay-making time, who got their biggest thrill out of riding on the lofty and precarious top of a stacked-up hayrack. What matter if they occasionally lost their balance and fell on a thistle in the hay? From this perch they could survey the wide world like small monarchs, and besides there was the wonderful smell of new-mown hay filling their

SPEAR'S PATENT CORN HUSKER

PORTER'S PATENT DERRICK

girls and engaged in tests of skill; the old men sat around and drank whisky out of jugs. The women prepared great repasts of game, pies, cakes, and puddings. The social gatherings were nearly all "work parties" during those laborious years and the "play party" did not reach its popularity until

SMALLEY'S SILO FILLER

FARM STEAM ENGINE

nostrils. Smalley's horse-powered apparatus for filling a silo was a team of horses operating a machine that ground corn and other silage. About the time Smalley introduced his apparatus the farm steam engine made its appearance in the central states region. Although it made a great racket and filled the virgin countryside with sulphurous smoke as it operated threshing and other machines, the steam engine replaced the horse as a source of power and remained in use until the coming of the Gasoline Age.

By now we have had enough of mechanical devices on farms during Grandfather's day. One might well ask: What of the social life, manners, modes, and morals of pioneer Midwesterners? One thing is certain: they were a sociable and co-operative race of people. At the husking bees, the house raisings, the log rollings, the apple parings, and the quilting parties, the work was done quickly and with a good deal of merriment. Afterward the young men "sparked" the

along about the middle of the century.

But there were shooting matches, wrestling bouts, foot marathons, and horse races, too, as well as more brutal sports, such as gander pullings, cock fights, and bull baitings. The horse races were not infrequently held in the main streets of villages, and pedestrians on these highways were wise to run for shelter when the sound of hoofbeats and the shouts of the racing men began. Sometimes ten or a dozen horsemen would start at one end of the street at the crack of a pistol and a minute or so later one of them would halt his quivering, sweating mare or stallion at a rope barrier stretched across the other end—the winner! While the sportsmen calculated their gains and losses, the timid "quiet folk" would emerge from their log houses or places of business and resume their trading and gossiping.

One of the most popular sources of entertainment in the backwoods country was the periodic court session conducted by the judge of a "circuit," which included several counties. People would come for miles by horseback or wagon, or even on foot, to the county seat to hear the august judge expound the mysteries of the law, the fine points of its technical and moral interpretation.

For religious services in the very earliest days and in remote backwoods sections, the settlers went to camp meetings, and these were even more exciting than political meetings. They were usually held at night, for a week or so, in a grove of trees lighted by candles, lamps, or torches. With hundreds of farmers and their families in attendance, these meetings, under the hell-and-damnation oratory of eloquent revivalist preachers, oftentimes reached a high emotional pitch. Shouting, shaking, and rolling on the ground frequently went with the "conversion" of listeners. One of the most famous of the backwoods exhorters was the itinerant preacher, Lorenzo Dow, who, wearing a Jesuslike beard, made the woods resound with the Word of God. Another early divine, perhaps even more colorful than the famous Reverend Lorenzo

JUDGES GOING TO COURT

[81]

CAMP MEETING

Dow, was the Reverend Peter Cartwright.

These outdoor religious meetings were continued long after the end of the log-cabin era. They were still going strong when, in the late 1850s, the Illinois Central Railroad advertised a kind of "prefabricated" cottage to newcomers buying land along its right of way in Illinois, offering for sale some 1,500,000 acres in tracts of forty acres and up "from $250 upwards."

MIDWEST COTTAGE

In a sense, this land-and-house bargain offer marks the decline of the buckskin-clad, cabin-dwelling pioneer and the beginning of a new era in Midwestern life. Schools and churches were built, colleges were founded, and agencies for social welfare were established. With the growing industrialization of the central states had arisen an ever-increasing number of homeless, helpless persons. The Civil War caused the break-up of many homes, throwing at large great numbers of dependent people. These, together with the technologically disestablished working class, which grew larger and larger with the practical application of labor-saving machinery, constituted a section of Midwestern humanity that had to be coped with as a serious problem. The polite word of the post-Civil War era for poorhouse or almshouse had become "eleemosynary institution," but the popular term, spoken always with dread, was still "poorhouse."

A poem that touched the hearts of our grandfathers and grandmothers was "Over the Hill to the Poor House." Here was a ballad that, although of Midwestern origin, brought a tear to the eyes of people all over America during the Sentimental Seventies. In almost all of the volumes of Will Carleton's verse, starting with *Farm Ballads,* first published in 1875, we find poems and ballads depicting many phases, grave and gay, of life in rural districts of the midland region during the mid-nineteenth century. It was Will Carleton who paved the way for that later folk poet of the region, James Whitcomb Riley.

With a stick and a small bag her sole worldly possessions, and casting a last back-

"OVER THE HILL"

"MANY A NIGHT I'VE WATCHED . . ."

ward glance toward her home, the old woman in "Over the Hill" is on her way to the poorhouse and has sad thoughts as she walks reluctantly along:

Over the hill to the poor-house I'm trudgin' my
    weary way—
I, a woman of seventy, and only a trifle gray—
I, who am smart an' chipper, for all the years
    I've told,
As many another woman that's only half as old.

On her way, she thinks again of the time when her children were babes, of the long silent nights when she sat up by lamplight rocking her young ones to sleep. Incidentally, part of the poorhouse which Will Carleton made famous in this verse still stands today in the small Michigan town of Hillsdale, seat of Hillsdale College. And

fifteen miles to the east of Hillsdale, there still exists the farmhouse in which Will Carleton was born and reared.

Not least among traditional events of mid-continental rural life celebrated by Will Carleton was the husking bee. It was the big social occasion of early autumn. The young people of the countryside would gather on a misty fall night and, by the light of lanterns, begin husking the ears of corn. As the work went on in the hay-smelling barn, there was much storytelling, singing of songs, exchange of gossip, and passing of rural badinage. Always, however, the young farmers were sharply on the lookout for a red ear of corn. To the finder of such an ear there came a high moment of the evening: the privilege of kissing the girl next to him. When work on the big pile of corn

THE HUSKING BEE

was finished, the floor was cleared of stalks and husks and a supper, perhaps of pork and beans, pumpkin pie, doughnuts, apples, and either hard or soft cider, was served. A neighborhood fiddler scraped tentatively on his ancient instrument, a caller went to the center of the barn, and the footsteps of a square dance shook the cobwebs on the shadowy rafters. But none of these delights of the husking bee could compare with the one that came when it was all over—riding

SINGING SCHOOL

OLD GUARD
OF THE WOODS

BAKING DAY

home in the buggy, by the light of a golden autumn moon with the girl of one's choice.

If the husking bee was something to look forward to among farm people, so was the village singing school. But we have the word of Will Carleton that the local sing-

ing master was almost forbidding in his whole-souled devotion to scales and notes:

Mr. Abraham Bates was a tune-stricken man,
Built on an exclusively musical plan;
With a body and soul that with naught could commune,
Unless it might somehow be set to a tune.

For the older folk in crossroads hamlets and rural villages of the region, a big event was the annual Old Settlers' Picnic. On such an occasion "The Old Guard of the Woods" recalled the days when newcomers to the West made clearings in the wilderness, built log cabins, and laid out farms. And sometimes at these picnics the graybeards got into heated arguments as they debated the year Banker Jones first came to

[85]

SCHOOL

THE RUNAWAY'S RETURN

their township "without a stitch on his back," or just where the cabin birthplace of Lawyer Woods was located.

There was a flavor and a savor to life in the region. And along with the smell of new-mown hay, freshly cut grass on a hot summer's night, burning leaves in autumn, and lilac blossoms in spring, there was that other most delightful of rural odors, the odor of bread just out of the oven. This smell was even more pleasurable when the plump brown loaves came out of a Dutch oven such as was used in the very earliest days. The children begged for one of the

fluffy rolls that usually were baked with the bread. Suffused with melting butter, a fresh roll of bread disappeared into the mouths of youngsters with almost digestion-impairing swiftness. And afterward there were wistful glances at the rows of loaves on the table, cooling under clean white towels.

The kitchen of a farm home, with its wonderful array of appetite-provoking odors, was a much more interesting place in which to tarry than the district school down at the crossroads. But there was no way out of the situation; the children had to go to school. And here, on winter days when the drifts were high and only a small, wood-burning stove tried bravely to warm the room, the "scholars" were put through their *McGuffey's Readers* by a stern schoolmaster, his authority re-enforced by a birch or hickory switch.

Sometimes, in spite of its manifold pleasures, tranquil home life in the rural districts became irksome to young people. Staying away from school, or running away from home, was the final resort of the discontented young. Oftentimes after a circus left town some fond country mother would be weeping over the disappearance of her boy. But she did not weep too hard. She knew that in a few days her son would begin to miss the odor of her hot bread, or the company of his pet dog. So she waited. Usually the prodigal would return, his face dirty, his clothes ragged, his stomach empty.

During the mellow, still days of fall, one could hear the far-off clatter of a horse-drawn reaper in some yellow grainfield, a sound that began in the crisp dawn and that ended in the afterglow of dusk. With the crops harvested, the silo filled, and the big red barn bulging with hay, the farmer could relax and enjoy some of the sports and social occasions of autumn.

As agriculture developed, there came into

being the annual country fair, with its exhibits of prize stock as well as its displays of preserves and finely designed bed quilts. One object always seen at the fair was the biggest pumpkin in the county. Later, the pumpkin would come into its own on Halloween. At this time youthful fingers would carve eyes and a nose in it and make a jack-o'-lantern to frighten casual wayfarers at night. But best of all were the Halloween parties, as popular then as now. With their witches on broomsticks, jack-o'-lanterns, apple dippings, and cider and doughnuts, these parties were the gayest of social affairs. Some young boys, however, preferred the more secretive pleasures of tipping over outhouses, removing gates, and indulging in other mischievous pranks.

As the prairie nights grew frostier than before, and a chill came into the autumn sunlight, the farmer began casting an appraising eye at some of the strutting turkey in his yard. One of them would be served on Thanksgiving Day, a big succulent bird, stuffed with sage or chestnut dressing and surrounded with cranberry sauce, mashed potatoes, apple pie, and all the other "fixin's." Finally, snow would whiten the fields and meadows, either falling silently and softly or coming in on the wings of a fierce blizzard. At last came the Christmas holidays. If the "front room" was a bit chilly on Christmas morning, youthful hearts were warmed by the wooden wagons and wax or china dolls and other toys that Santa Claus had brought. And the occasion was made even more glamorous as, with the coming of the winter dusk, the children lighted the candles on the tinsel-decorated tree.

But life on the farms was not all festivals, holidays, and social occasions. The farmers worked hard and had to struggle in a continuous battle against droughts, blizzards,

HARVEST TIME

A PUMPKIN FOR THE FAIR

floods, prairie fires, and insect plagues.

And then there was that sudden and most terrible of all scourges of the Midwestern flatlands, the tornado. Storms were fearsome occurrences to dwellers in makeshift cottages or cabins in the wilderness, and even well-to-do farmers in their stoutly built homes were often completely ruined by a cyclone.

If one lived in open country, he could see the fearful funnel-shaped cloud coming and could hurry his family into the cyclone cellar, if he had one. But dwellers in towns, with their shade trees, houses, and other

[87]

TORNADO

VICTORIAN MIDWEST PARLOR

obstructions to view, could not always observe the approach of a tornado.

Tornadoes, fortunately, did not often strike twice in the same place. And as wealth grew from fields and factories, the sons and daughters of the pioneer settlers achieved a sense of good living that lifted them above the fear of upheavals of nature. They acquired lightning rods and storm cellars and they constructed their houses very solidly.

In these commodious homes, dwellings with such exterior appurtenances of the time as wide porches, ornamental cupolas, bulging bay windows, and scrollwork eave brackets, the well-to-do descendants of the early settlers were surrounded with all the comfortable, if stuffy, household furnishings of the late Victorian era. A good many of the middle-class parlors of the period were almost alike in their appointments. Walking from the parlor into the kitchen of the house, especially on a washday, you perhaps would have found one of those new-fangled contraptions, a "Universal Clothes Wringer," in operation, squeezing out dripping sheets and pillow cases from a wooden washtub into a wicker clothesbasket.

If such were the comforts of a typical farm home in the years just after the Civil War, there came a time when these comforts were threatened. In the early 1870s, the farmers of the Wheat Belt found themselves in economic distress through no fault of their own. Having the blood of resourceful pioneers in their veins, they did something about this situation. They started the Granger Movement. This was the beginning of what later became the Populist Movement in the Midwest and which produced such prairie leaders as William Jennings Bryan and Ignatius Donnelly. When the Granger Movement, fostered by the

CLOTHES WRINGER

GRANGE MEETING

[89]

"Housekeepers' Improvement Club"

National Grange of the Patrons of Husbandry, was in full swing throughout the Central States, the farmers and their wives and neighbors, calling themselves "Grangers," adopted plans for concerted political action at meetings in district schoolhouses and local halls. As the result of such a widespread uprising of the farm population, economic conditions in the Wheat Belt were bettered. One objective which the Grangers achieved was a more reasonable scale of railroad-freight rates than formerly. With the farmer's economic status thus improved, and with his continued success in the growing and marketing of crops,

Texas Buggy

a bid was soon made for his trade and custom by the Chicago wholesale firm of Montgomery Ward and Company, and here we have the birth of that familiar Midwestern institution, the mail-order house. The business of this firm, as well as that of Sears, Roebuck and Company, expanded greatly after the parcel-post system was inaugurated by the government in 1912.

Although the era of women's clubs was not yet at hand, women of the early 1880s had one medium for the exchange of ideas in the "Housekeepers' Improvement Club," a column in the pages of the *Prairie Farmer*. Could the editor of this column have had his tongue in his cheek when he wrote an introductory paragraph? It read: "These meetings take the form of familiar conversations, much of which is necessarily omitted by the Secretary, her aim being to catch and note down such items as may seem to be of most general interest. The chat at any meeting, if reported literally or in full, would occupy a dozen columns, and require a skillful and rapid stenographer."

No account of Midwestern life in days gone by would be complete without some reference to one of the most familiar and most appreciated objects of that time, the four-wheeled Texas buggy. Here was an almost universal mode of conveyance before the "horseless carriage" era. Washed thoroughly with the garden hose before each trip to town, the Texas buggy, pulled by a lively bay, carried our parents or grandparents with some degree of comfort along bumpy country roads. In turning street corners in town, though, they had to be careful not to make too sharp a turn, or else the front wheel would upset the buggy. At the hitching post in the Courthouse Square, Grandpa found dozens of other Texas buggies tied up, as well as fringed-topped surreys, buckboards, and of course green-painted Springfield wagons. After Grandpa's session with some of the "boys" around the cracker barrel and Grandma's shopping spree in the general store, the two started back home again in the buggy. If a few drops indicated a coming rainstorm, Grandpa got out the storm curtains and attached them to the buggy hood. Once more back in the farmyard, Grandpa would find his buggy (barring rain) covered with dust, which meant another washing before the next trip to town, or to church.

IN THE LAND OF LINCOLN

ON AN autumn day in 1816, a Kentucky backwoodsman and his wife and two children ferried across the Ohio River at Anderson Creek. That backwoodsman brought to the Midwest a boy who became inland America's greatest man.

When Tom Lincoln and his wife, Nancy, crossed the Ohio on that chilly day, their son, Abe, was seven years old. Their daughter, Sarah, was nine. On their wagon were some eight or ten "bar'ls" of whisky which Tom Lincoln had received in trade for his Kentucky farm, whisky in those days being a kind of legal tender. After a two-day journey through the Indiana forests, the Lincolns arrived at their claim on Little Pigeon Creek, near the present-day town of Gentryville. The following spring they erected a rude cabin in which Abraham Lincoln began a Midwestern career which did not come to an end until, as President-elect of the United States, a train bore him away from his adopted town of Springfield, Illinois.

The Ohio River was to Abe a glimpse of the outside world. He afterward came often to the Anderson Creek hamlet and when he was sixteen got a job there as a ferryman. But first he was a woodsman. At an early age he also learned to farm.

Two years after the Lincolns had settled in the little clearing on Pigeon Creek, the "milk sick" visited the region. Nancy Lincoln succumbed and died. Her death made a deep, disturbing impression on the sensitive mind of the boy.

A miserable, cheerless winter followed. A little more than a year later, however, after a quick trip to Kentucky, Tom Lincoln returned to Indiana with a new wife, the widowed Sarah Bush Johnston, and her three children.

An energetic, capable woman, possessed of intelligence and understanding, the new Mrs. Lincoln was quick to see Abe Lincoln's desire for knowledge and urged her husband to let the boy read all the books he could get his hands on. But Tom Lincoln did not care for "book larnin'." Such at least was his attitude until a neighbor bargained to buy a small part of the Lincoln farm. When this neighbor wrote a deed and presented it to Tom Lincoln to sign, the younger Lincoln, knowing his father could not read, asked to see it. "If you sign this, you've sold the whole farm," said Abe to his father. Tom Lincoln looked at the neighbor and said: "Somebody's lied and 'taint Abe!" Whereupon a fist fight followed, ending with Tom Lincoln the victor. After this event, Tom Lincoln no longer objected to "book larnin'."

Not far from the Lincoln home stood the Pigeon Creek Baptist Church, a rude log meetinghouse which Tom Lincoln helped to build. Subscriptions for the support of the church were paid for in farm products and Thomas Lincoln is entered in the records as having contributed twenty-four pounds of "manufactured" corn. This was probably corn meal prepared at the local gristmill. In those days, it was customary for each farmer to use his own horse in turning the mill wheel. One day Abe drove an "old flea-bitten gray mare" to the mill. As he was in a hurry, he used a whip on the slow-moving mare and continually shouted at it, "Get up, you old hussy!" Suddenly the old mare lifted her hoofs and struck Abe in the forehead, knocking him to the ground. Hurried home in a wagon, the boy remained unconscious all night. This accident, which might have been fatal, was often referred to by Lincoln in later life.

Although Abe went to school at intervals, the total sum of his time spent there would hardly amount to a year. Mostly he educated himself by what few books he could borrow.

As he approached young manhood, becoming taller each year, Abe Lincoln got restless. He wanted to break away from the drudgery of backwoods life. When James

LINCOLN CABIN, GENTRYVILLE, INDIANA

ANDERSON CREEK FERRY

PIGEON CREEK CHURCH

[93]

FIRST LINCOLN HOME IN ILLINOIS

SECOND LINCOLN HOME IN ILLINOIS

Gentry, the leading merchant of Gentryville, asked nineteen-year-old Abe if he would like to take a flatboat full of grain and meat to New Orleans, the young man from Pigeon Creek welcomed the opportunity. And so Abe Lincoln and the merchant's son, Allen, went down the Ohio and the Mississippi on a flatboat. In New Orleans young Abe Lincoln saw Negro slaves being sold at auction and this stirred him deeply.

When he returned to his Indiana clearing, Abe found that his entire family was becoming restless. They, too, wanted to be "on the move." They had heard about the rich lands of Illinois and felt that state was a better place for them than Indiana. On a March day in 1830, when Abe had already reached the age of twenty-one, the Lincolns, riding in a heavy wagon drawn by two yoke of oxen, headed westward. Just behind the wagon walked the family's pet dog. One day, after fording a river with cakes of ice in it, they discovered their dog still on the other side of the river, whining and showing signs of being afraid. Anxious to be on their way, the family decided to abandon the animal. At this point, however, Abe Lincoln jumped out of the wagon. "I could not endure the idea of abandoning even a dog," said Lincoln, in telling the story. "Pulling off shoes and socks I waded across the stream and triumphantly returned with the shivering animal. . . . His frantic leaps of joy and other evidences of a dog's gratitude amply repaid me."

After crossing the Wabash River at the old French town of Vincennes, the Lincolns entered Illinois and made their slow way across the prairie grasslands to a point on the Sangamon River some eight miles from the city of Decatur. Here work was immediately begun on a cabin and on cultivation of the claim. For fencing here, Abe and his cousin, John Hanks, split hundreds of rails, some of which, according to legend, were later found and displayed in the Lincoln presidential campaign. A year after settling at this point, the Lincolns moved once more, this time to a tract of land near the present city of Mattoon, Illinois. A new log house was built. It was here that Abe Lincoln said good-by to his sturdy old pioneering father and kindly stepmother and went out into the wide-spreading Midwestern world of log settlements, county-seat court-houses, river flatboats, and overland trails.

Lanky, thoughtful-eyed Abe Lincoln decided to settle in the recently founded village of New Salem, located some eighteen miles northwest of the then obscure town of Springfield. He arrived in New Salem on Election Day. A crowd of citizens from near and far filled the polling place and the clerk was hard-pressed. When it was found that Lincoln, who loitered on the edge of the crowd, could write, he was immediately placed in service as clerk's assistant. Thus it was that Abraham Lincoln began his political career in the log settlement of New Salem, a career that was to take him to the White House and immortality.

New Salem eventually was deserted and became a "ghost town," with only the ruins of the Onstot cooper shop surviving, and no pictorial record of its appearance during Lincoln's time or later was ever made. Some idea of the layout of the village, however, may be gotten from an old map prepared for William H. Herndon, one-time law partner of Lincoln's and one of his early biographers. This map shows a typical frontier settlement, with gristmill, general store, and a dozen or so homes. Here Lincoln whipped the champion bully of the countryside, became a store clerk, a captain in the Black Hawk War, a postmaster, a surveyor, a law student, and finally a state legislator. Here he fell in love with auburn-haired Ann Rutledge. And when this romance came to a tragic end with the death of Ann, it left a shadow on the soul of Abraham Lincoln that remained there for the rest of his days. After she was buried, Lincoln, in speaking of her grave, told a friend: "My heart lies there."

Not far away from New Salem (now restored as a historic shrine) stands the town of Petersburg, a community that grew up with the decline of New Salem. In the courthouse at Petersburg a Congressional Convention of the Whig Party, meeting in 1846, nominated Lincoln as its candidate for Congress. When the Democratic Party named the Reverend Peter Cartwright, a famous circuit-riding preacher of the time, a lively campaign followed. Not wanting to mix politics with religion, the voters

chose Lincoln and the tall prairie lawyer entered for the first time on the scene of national political life. Earlier, when Lincoln was first elected to the Illinois Legislature in 1834, the state capital was at Vandalia, an old town in southern Illinois. Still standing today in that town is the ancient state-capitol building in which Lincoln served as a representative from 1834 to 1839. During that time there was issued in this building, on March 4, 1837, the city charter of Chicago, which was then but a straggling town of log and frame houses clustered around Fort Dearborn. In this building, too, Lincoln headed the "Long Nine," a group of six-foot legislators which brought about removal of the state capital to Springfield.

NEW SALEM, ILLINOIS

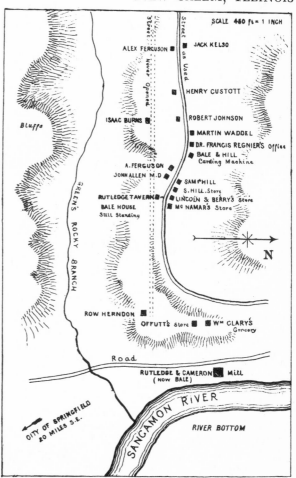

[95]

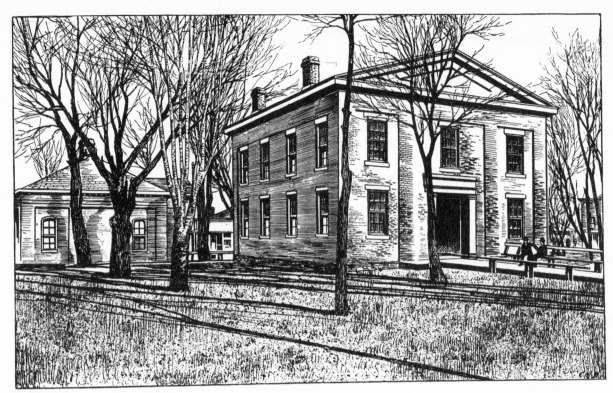

Petersburg Court House

Old State House, Vandalia

When this happened, Lincoln himself became a resident of Springfield and remained there as a lawyer and public official until his election to the presidency. As an attorney in Springfield, Lincoln often appeared before the State Supreme Court, the chamber of which was in the new state capitol. In this building on a day in 1858, was held a convention of the state Republican Party at which Lincoln was nominated for United States Senator. Immediately after the nomination, the delegates called for a speech from their candidate. Lincoln delivered his famous "House Divided" speech, an address that wound up with the fateful words: " 'A house divided against itself cannot stand.' I believe this government cannot endure permanently half slave and half free." Only once more did the dignified Greek Revival statehouse at Springfield, Illinois, shelter the man who delivered the "House Divided" speech within its walls. This time that man was dead and, as a martyred President of the United States, his body lay in state here.

When Lincoln was a practicing attorney in Springfield, he formed successive partnerships with three of the leading lawyers of that city. Shortly after becoming a resident there, he associated himself with John T. Stuart and opened an office just across the street from the statehouse. Then, in 1841, he formed a partnership with Stephen T. Logan and set up an office at 203 South Sixth Street. In 1844 Lincoln became associated with William H. Herndon and this lasted until the former left Springfield for the White House.

Where now Illinois's great Centennial Building stands there once was located the imposing residence of Ninian W. Edwards, Territorial Governor of Illinois. On a

OLD STATE HOUSE, SPRINGFIELD

November day in 1842 this house was the scene of the marriage of Abraham Lincoln to Mary Todd, sister-in-law of Governor Edwards. The Lincolns were not financially able to build a home of their own, and lived for the first two years of their married life in the Globe Tavern. Writing of this period to a friend, Lincoln said: "We are not keeping house, but boarding at the Lincoln was officially notified of his nomination as a presidential candidate, being waited upon by a committee of distinguished citizens from Chicago, where the Republican Convention had been held in the Wigwam. And it was in the "sitting-room" of this Eighth Street dwelling that the lanky master of the house stretched out his long legs, relaxed, and romped with his boys.

LINCOLN'S LAW OFFICES AT SPRINGFIELD

Globe Tavern, which is very well kept now by a widow lady of the name of Beck. Our room . . . and boarding only costs us four dollars a week."

Eventually the Lincolns bought a home of their own, the one on Eighth Street which today is one of the most important historic shrines of the Midwest. It was in the south parlor of this house that Abraham

While Lincoln was being nominated for the presidency at Chicago, he was nervously waiting for news in Springfield. At the office of the *Springfield Journal* he learned from a telegraph messenger that his nomination had taken place. As may be observed from a portrait of him made at the time he did not then wear the beard which became such a familiar facial adornment after he

WHERE LINCOLN WAS MARRIED

LINCOLN RESIDENCE IN SPRINGFIELD

PARLOR OF LINCOLN RESIDENCE

went to the White House in Washington.

Some nine months after this event, President-elect Abraham Lincoln said good-by to his fellow Springfieldians at the town's railroad station. His parting words were: "My friends! No one not in my situation can appreciate my feeling of sadness at this

GLOBE TAVERN

LINCOLN SITTING ROOM

[99]

ABRAHAM LINCOLN IN 1860

parting. To this place and the kindness of these people I owe everything. Here I have lived a quarter of a century, and have passed from a young man to an old man. Here my children have been born, and one of them is buried. I now leave, not knowing when or whether ever I may return, with a task before me greater than that which rested upon Washington. Without the assistance of that Divine Being who ever attended him, I cannot succeed. With that assistance, I cannot fail. Trusting in Him, Who can go with me, and remain with you, and be everywhere for good, let us confidently hope that all will yet be well. To His care commending you, as I hope in your prayers you will commend me, I bid you an affectionate farewell."

President Lincoln never again saw the Midwest. It was as a martyred President that he was brought back and laid to rest in the soil that nurtured him, that gave him the thoughts and dreams which made of him a man of the ages.

Once more back in his beloved Springfield, Abraham Lincoln was buried in Oak Ridge Cemetery, and above his last resting place was erected a monument that would honor his memory for as long a time as granite lasted.

THE NATIONAL ROAD

ALONG that part of U. S. 40 which runs through central Ohio, the motorist comes upon mileposts, very ancient wayside inns, now and then a venerable tollhouse, and quite often a curious S-shaped bridge, surviving evidences of the famous old National Road. Built more than 150 years ago and the Midwest's first great overland highway, lengthened from time to time until it reached Indiana and Illinois, the National Road followed the Ohio River as the second most important route of travel into the interior of America.

Numerous villages and towns sprang up along the National Road, and many of these evolved into cities, including Ohio's state capital, Columbus. Of similar origin are Cambridge, Zanesville, and Springfield. Even Dayton was substantially aided in its growth by the National Road. After this wagon trail was extended to Indiana, a sharp increase in population was noted. The further extension of the road to Illinois quickened the pulse of life in early Illinois villages.

This historic turnpike was first known as Zane's Trace. In the spring of 1796 legislation was passed by Congress authorizing Ebenezer Zane to open a road through the forests of the Ohio country. In the work Zane was aided by his brother, Jonathan Zane, and by his son-in-law, John McIntire. Although hardly more than a trail for horsemen, Zane's Trace afterward became a much-traveled roadway.

In 1825 Ebenezer Zane's old turnpike became part of the National Road, which also had absorbed the old Cumberland Road from Cumberland, Maryland, to Wheeling, West Virginia. As the National

Road was extended farther westward, Conestoga wagons, packhorse trains, horsemen, and even droves of cattle, and pigs, traveled on its graded, crushed-stone surface. The lumbering Conestoga wagon, usually pulled by a six-horse team, was a colorful object on the National Road as its white canopy, blue body, and red wheels stood out in contrast to other vehicles.

Sometimes pioneers traveling along the National Road would form their covered wagons into caravans, or wagon trains, for the sake of mutual help. Not all of the wagons were drawn by horses. Almost as often one could see wagons pulled by a yoke or two of slow-moving oxen. The owner of the wagon usually guided his team on foot, but sometimes he rode a horse. The members of his family were a tired, dusty lot at sundown when they turned off the National Road to pitch camp. After unharnessing the horses, the "mover" would start a fire and his wife would busy herself among the pots and pans. Most of these families entered the western country at Bridgeport just across the Ohio River from Wheeling. Bridgeport was called the gateway to Ohio.

On a March day in 1837, when the National Road was at the peak of its career, there was born at Martins Ferry a boy who was given the name of William Dean Howells. It was a curious character of this region, Joseph Dylkes, who gave Howells the inspiration for *The Leatherwood God*.

Quite often, wagon trains on Zane's Trace and the National Road carried migrant bodies of religious sects. Over the original trace came a group of Quakers who were among the first settlers of Saint Clairsville. One of their number, a young saddler

COVERED WAGON

PIONEER CAMP

BIRTHPLACE OF WILLIAM DEAN HOWELLS

BENJAMIN LUNDY

named Benjamin Lundy, formed an anti-slavery organization called the Union Humane Society. Membership in his society grew quickly and he became the founder of the abolitionist movement in the Midwest.

In order to obtain revenue for the upkeep of the National Road, toll gates were set up. One such toll station was at Morristown.

The rate varied according to the amount of damage caused the road by vehicles and animals. In 1837 the fee for a coach-and-four was twenty-five cents, while wagons were assessed from ten to twenty cents and a horse and rider taxed three cents. When the National Road reached its peak year of traffic in Ohio in 1839 the amount of revenue derived from tolls was considerably

PENNYROYAL DISTILLERY

most difficult type of bridge they could think of. Another type of bridge was the covered bridge. One such served the road at Cambridge, west of Middlebourne. Before this bridge existed, and on the day the town was laid out, there arrived a group of families from the Isle of Guernsey. When a county was formed in this region it was given the name of Guernsey.

At Zanesville stage passengers found one

CAMBRIDGE, OHIO

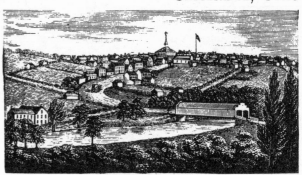

more than sixty-two thousand dollars.

A medicinal herb much used by early settlers in the wilderness was pennyroyal and there grew up, along the National Road near Fairview, an extensive pennyroyal-distilling industry. This industry had its beginnings among farmers of the area, who gathered pennyroyal, distilled it, and shipped it to the National Road.

There exists today near Middlebourne one of those curious S-shaped bridges which were such familiar sights on the early turnpike. One version of this origin has it that they were so constructed to stop runaway horses, another that two freely imbibing engineers dared each other to construct the

MCINTIRE'S HOTEL, ZANESVILLE, OHIO

of the most comfortable early roadside taverns, McIntire's Hotel. This building was a great improvement over what had previously existed in Zanesville. John McIntire, Ebenezer Zane's son-in-law, provided beds and a generous board. A distinguished guest at McIntire's Hotel in those days was the exiled Louis Philippe, afterward King of France.

For several years before the opening of the National Road, Zanesville was the capital of Ohio. Later the capitol building in Zanesville became the Muskingum County Courthouse. Zanesville achieved fame not only for its unique "Y" bridge but as the manufacturing place of unusually fine pottery work.

Soon after the close of the Civil War, there passed through Zanesville, on the old National Road, a wagon train that was perhaps the biggest in history. Several thousand of General Sherman's army wagons rattled through on their way to posts beyond the Mississippi. This caravan required several weeks to pass through.

Columbus was an important stop on the National Road, a transfer point between stages on the National Road and those traveling north-south routes. As a consequence, there was built at Columbus the famous Neil House, a hostelry and also the headquarters of Neil, Moore and Company, a leading stagecoach line of the period.

After blowing on his brass horn, the driver of a stage would bring his team up before the entrance of the Neil House. In the hotel the passengers were assigned rooms and fed at a long table. Afterward they could partake of the liquid refreshments of the taproom. In the morning there would be a fresh four-horse team attached

ZANESVILLE IN 1846

to their stage to continue the journey.

When the Neil House was destroyed by fire, it was replaced by a larger hostelry of the same name, which survived even after railroad lines displaced the stagecoach. Both old and new hotels were frequented by state officials and politicians for the Neil House was across from the state capitol. Although work on this building was started in 1839, it was not completed until 1861.

Ohio State University, located at Colum-

bus, was opened in 1873. A few years after the National Road had changed Springfield from an obscure village to a bustling highway town, Wittenberg College, one of the oldest Midwest colleges, was established there by the Lutheran Church.

There was much whisky drinking in taverns along the National Road, and also a temperance movement. One stage line, the Good Intent Line, had been established by a very ardent temperance leader, General N. P. Talmadge. He even urged passengers using his line to desist from the use of strong liquors. But General Talmadge always provided comfortable coaches and kept to his schedules.

Some of the ladies of Springfield dramatized the temperance movement in a novel way. Says an 1874 issue of *Frank Leslie's Illustrated Newspaper*: "A band of women enter a saloon, and ask that it be closed. If this is refused, they ask permission to hold a prayer-meeting, and if this is denied they retire to the sidewalk and hold meetings until the man yields."

Traffic on the old National Road was already beginning to decline when Antioch College was founded at Yellow Springs in

ZANESVILLE, 1880

[105]

SHERMAN'S WAGONS

STATE CAPITOL AT COLUMBUS

OHIO STATE UNIVERSITY

WITTENBERG COLLEGE

ANTIOCH COLLEGE

COLUMBUS IN 1846

COLUMBUS IN THE 1880s

DAYTON IN THE 1840s

SECOND STATE HOUSE, INDIANAPOLIS

DAYTON, 1890

STATE BANK, INDIANAPOLIS

"THE OHIO WHISKY WAR"

1853. The first president of this institution was Horace Mann, who fought to set up at Antioch a college free from sectarian influence. Before his death, Horace Mann saw his plan in successful operation.

In its earliest days, Dayton supplied many passengers to stages on the turnpike, although the road was located some ten miles north of the settlement. The birthplace of the cash register, Dayton was also the headquarters of the Driggs Gang, one of the most notorious cash-counterfeiting gangs in American history, which flourished in the 1880s and was broken up by the United States Secret Service.

By the time the National Road reached Indiana, its operation had been turned over to the various states along its route. Indiana leased its portion to a private company. It is said that laborers worked on this part of the road from dawn to dark for fifty cents

a day. By 1850 the road extended clear across the state.

On arrival at Indianapolis, stage passengers found a lively town with handsome buildings, most of them designed in the prevailing Greek Revival style. Of outstanding importance was the State Capitol, completed in 1834.

Another distinctive building of the Hoosier capital was the Indiana State Bank. Many citizens of Indianapolis also pointed with pride to the Masonic Temple. Of more interest than any of these buildings, however, would be the Union Depot. For a while it looked as though Indianapolis was destined to become the railroad capital of the world.

About sixty miles northwest of Indianapolis, on the outskirts of the city of Lafayette, lies the ground on which was fought the Battle of Tippecanoe, the winning of which on November 7, 1811, brought fame to General William Henry Harrison. It also gave him a campaign slogan in the noisy "Log Cabin and Hard Cider" presidential race of 1840: "Tippecanoe and Tyler too!" Worn out by this tumultuous campaign, General Harrison died in the White House one month after being inaugurated.

Other passengers that arrived in Indianap-

INDIANAPOLIS MASONIC TEMPLE

UNION DEPOT, INDIANAPOLIS

INDIANA STATE UNIVERSITY

olis were students bound for Indiana State University, at Bloomington, and Wabash College, at Crawfordsville. The former began as a seminary in 1820 and the latter started operations in 1833. In 1874 Indiana's other renowned university, Purdue, was founded at Lafayette.

As he traveled on the National Road west of Indianapolis, the stage passenger would observe a rolling countryside containing great tracts of winter wheat. Thus the stage would bump all day over the muddy planks of the turnpike until it arrived at Terre Haute. After crossing the Wabash River at Terre Haute, the National Road entered Illinois.

Not many stage passengers would be likely to leave the Indiana side of the Na-

WABASH COLLEGE

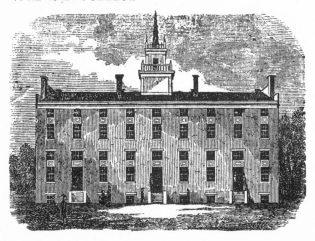

PURDUE UNIVERSITY

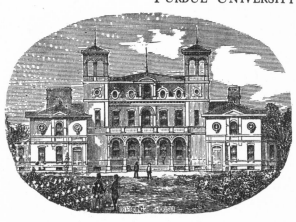

tional Road, however, without hearing from someone the story of how ex-President Martin Van Buren was dumped into a mudhole on the turnpike at the Indiana village of Plainfield. The episode happened on a June day in 1842 when the ex-President was making a swing around the country in preparation for entering the 1844 presidential campaign. On his arrival at Plainfield, the dapper, dignified Martin Van Buren was thrown into a muddy ditch when his stagecoach overturned. According to the lore of the old turnpike, this "accident" was deliberately arranged by Plainfield citizens. They were resentful of Martin Van Buren, who had vetoed a bill for improvement of the National Road. The driver of the Van Buren stage, Mason Wright, said he received a silk hat for his part in the affair.

ALONG THE OHIO

ON A RAINY morning in 1788, a group of unshaven men on a barnlike flatboat, drifting down the Ohio River, nearly missed their destination, the mouth of the Muskingum River. The land along the north bank of the Ohio, for miles and miles, was their own land. They possessed a domain of no less than 1,500,000 acres in this wilderness region that later became the southeastern corner of the state of Ohio. They could have landed anywhere along this reach of the north bank of the Ohio and been on ground to which they had title. But these flatboatmen, determined New Englanders, were set on finding the mouth of the Muskingum, the gateway to their new domain in the western country.

The fog made it all but impossible for them to locate the river mouth. Consequently, they drifted along in the stillness and would have gone much farther downstream had not something in the mist attracted their attention. They decided to stop. Climbing up the steep bank, they were welcomed by loud cheers from some soldiers and learned that chance had led them to their destination.

These flatboatmen were the Pilgrim Fathers of the Midwest. The spot where they landed, and the region round about it, was a mysterious, Indian-trod wilderness. The French had earlier explored and claimed this vast level region lying west of the Alleghenies, and the British had afterward acquired it only to lose it to the newborn American republic, yet it had remained largely unsettled by the white race until the arrival of those shivering flatboatmen.

These men, after establishing a settlement which they called "Marietta," in honor of Queen Marie Antoinette and French aid during the Revolution, were the first to set up a civil government in "The West" under the American flag. This government embraced the region out of which were later carved the states of Ohio, Indiana, Illinois, Michigan, Wisconsin, and part of Minnesota. These states, founded on a broad base of democracy, gave form and substance to the later Midwest, Missouri, Iowa, Kansas, Nebraska, South Dakota and North Dakota.

If this great area was early known as "The West," it was also called "The Northwest." Geographers could not agree on a suitable name for such a vaguely defined part of the country. The designation "Northwest" arose from the fact that it lay northwest of Virginia. When the men on the flatboat came to their destination on April 7, 1788, they had with them documents from Congress authorizing them to settle in "The Northwest Territory."

Not only did the New England flatboatmen find evidence of lurking Indians, but they discovered a prehistoric mound, which still stands today in Marietta, forming the centerpiece of Mound Cemetery, in which are interred the remains of many of the leading founders of the colony.

On the flatboat were carpenters, shipbuilders, and surveyors. Altogether there were forty-eight of them and they were in

PIONEERS ON THE OHIO

reality distributed on a flotilla of two big flatboats and five pirogues. As some of these men were intellectually inclined and somewhat prone to argue small points, difficulty was encountered in arriving at a proper name for their big, awkward leading boat. This craft was variously known as the *Adventure Galley,* the *Union Galley,* and the *American Mayflower.* In command of these original "Buckeyes" was General Rufus Putnam, an outstanding engineer on Washington's staff during the Revolution, and a cousin of General Israel Putnam, also of Revolutionary fame. It was General Rufus Putnam who, with the Reverend Manasseh Cutler, originated a plan for the settlement of the new country in the "Territory of the United States North and West of the River Ohio."

To carry out this plan, Putnam and Cutler called a meeting of former Revolutionary War soldiers at the Bunch of Grapes Tavern in Boston on March 1, 1786, and brought about formation of the Ohio Company of Associates, organized to purchase land in the new western country. That was in the days when Boston taverns served a. civic centers. At the 1786 conference General Putnam was elected superintendent of the group and the Reverend Mr. Cutler, a lawyer and a physician as well as a minister, was chosen as its land-purchasing agent.

A year later the minister went before the Continental Congress and succeeded in obtaining from that body a tract of 1,500,-000 acres along the Ohio and Muskingum rivers. For payment, the men of the Ohio Company of Associates offered their military certificates, which were accepted. At that time these certificates were greatly depreciated, so that the men of the Ohio Company actually paid not more than eight cents an acre for their land. Grateful to Dr. Cutler for this purchase, the men of the

RUFUS PUTNAM

MANASSEH CUTLER

Company were now ready to move westward to their new claim.

But before this could be done, civil government had to be established in the huge region that had been won from the British by George Rogers Clark. As a matter of fact, it had been established just before the Ohio Company made its purchase, having been effectuated by the famous Ordinance of 1787, which created the Northwest Territory. One who had an important hand in the creation of that ordinance was Thomas Jefferson and in 1784 he had envisioned in the new region seven additional states to the Union, even going so far as to give them such classical names as Polypotamia, Sylvania, Polisipia, Chersonesus, Assenisipia, Michigania, and Metropotamia.

Said to contain many provisions suggested by Putnam, Cutler, and other leaders of the Ohio Company of Associates, the Ordinance of 1787 embraced such significantly democratic principles as the forbidding of slavery in the Territory, the setting aside of tax-free lands for schools, universities, and churches, freedom of speech, press, and assembly, and the right of citizens to vote regardless of whether or not they owned land. These were the principles that the hardy men on the flatboat brought with them, principles that became the foundation stones of Midwestern civilization.

Previous to the arrival of this advance guard of the Ohio Company of Associates, the tremendous area of the new western country, stretching from the Alleghenies to the Mississippi and from the Great Lakes to the Ohio River, had been under the control of the military, which accounted for a fort at such a strategic location as the confluence of the Ohio and Muskingum rivers. Called Fort Harmar, it had been built two

INAUGURATION OF TERRITORIAL GOVERNMENT AT MARIETTA

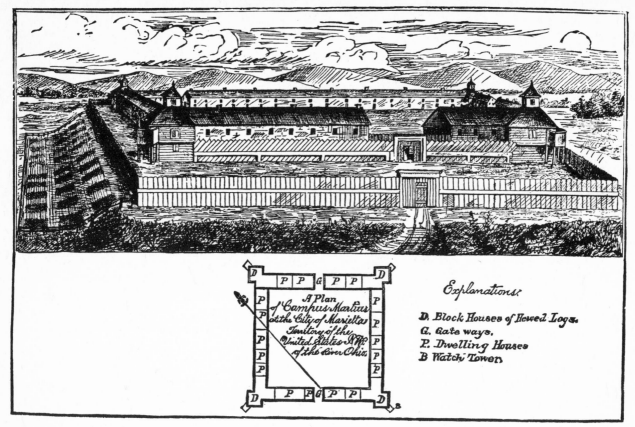

CAMPUS MARTIUS

or three years before the arrival of the flat-boatmen. The territory's first governor was Arthur Saint Clair. The inauguration ceremonies took place on the 15th of July, 1788.

Marietta became the first legal settlement of the Northwest Territory. Before their ample hearth fires here, some of these men could recall that cold December dawn of the year before when the first group of them left Ipswich, Massachusetts. These were boatbuilders and carpenters, who planned on being in the Ohio Country by spring in order to start building houses. Assembled at daybreak before the Reverend Mr. Cutler's parsonage on December 3, 1787, the men listened to the minister's parting words of cheer, jumped into their covered wagon, and in a few moments were creaking on their way westward. On the canvas hood of

their wagon Dr. Cutler had painted the words: For the OHIO COUNTRY.

After an eight weeks' journey they came to Sumrill's Ferry, where now stands West Newton, Pennsylvania. There they got out their saws and axes and, despite winter snows, began building flatboats and pirogues for the Ohio River passage and there they were later joined by a party of surveyors and mechanics under General Putnam. Finally, on April 1, 1788, all forty-eight of these New Englanders embarked on the Ohio and arrived seven days later at the mouth of the haze-obscured Muskingum.

The settlement they built at this point, under the supervision of the military engineer General Putnam, was unique for the frontier. It was both stronghold and village.

[115]

FLOOD AT MARIETTA

There was still danger from Indian attack and these colonists had to be prepared for any emergency. They therefore built a 180-foot-square stockade of stout logs. The four walls of the enclosure consisted of the homes of the colonists. Into these crude but comfortable homes, the men of the Ohio Company later brought their wives and children. They named their somewhat medieval-looking stronghold "Campus Martius." It was a true "Field of Mars": a place where they could quickly transform themselves into soldiers.

This fortified village became not only a residing place for the settlers but the capital of the Northwest Territory. Here Governor Arthur Saint Clair established his headquarters; here were held the first Sunday school, first day school, and first town meeting in the territory; and here were welcomed many well-known travelers in the western country, including the exiled Duke of Orléans, Louis Philippe, who afterward became King of France. Another guest here was Harman Blennerhassett, later to become involved with Aaron Burr in his conspiracy. Most welcome of all, however, was the Reverend Mr. Cutler, who drove all the way from Ipswich in a sulky.

After the Battle of Fallen Timbers in 1794, when "Mad Anthony" Wayne decisively defeated the Indians, the westward movement of immigrants gained added momentum and the men of the Marietta colony were now free to go out into the great woods north of the Ohio and stake out their claims on the 1,500,000-acre tract secured for them by the Reverend Mr. Cutler. Their axes soon were making clearings in the virgin forest. In time the Muskingum Valley was dotted with cabins and farms.

Meanwhile, their original settlement of Marietta grew and prospered, became an important river port and shipbuilding center, and by the time of the Civil War was a good-sized city. But sometimes there were temporary setbacks to Marietta's progress, such as Ohio River floods. Usually occurring after the melting of the snows in spring, these floods would at first cause alarm among Mariettans, many of them fleeing panic-stricken to higher land. After the peak of the flood stage was reached, and

out in 1797 by Bezaleel Wells and James Ross. Bezaleel Wells seems to have been the "father" of industrial Steubenville, having introduced merino sheep into the region at an early day and, in 1814, opened a wool-cloth plant. Once the wealthiest person in that part of the country, Bezaleel Wells died a poor man.

About fifty miles west of Steubenville occurred, not a massacre of whites by In-

MARKET STREET, STEUBENVILLE

it was seen there was no loss of life and not too much property damage, Mariettans breathed more easily.

Some Midwest historians claim that Steubenville, that now thriving steel town on the Ohio River, is an older community than Marietta, pointing out that a settlement grew up here around Fort Steuben as early as 1787. Whatever the merits of this claim, Steubenville certainly grew quickly. Actually, the town itself was formally laid

dians, but a terrible massacre of Indians by whites. This slaughter was all the more hideous because the ninety-six Indians killed here, men, women, and children, were unarmed and peaceful. Said to have been aroused by a number of supposedly Indian-committed murders in the vicinity, Captain David Williamson and a group of militiamen crossed the Pennsylvania border and entered Ohio on the morning of March 7, 1782, heading for near-by Gnadenhutten,

[117]

a peaceful colony of Indians who had been converted to the Christian faith by the pioneer Moravian missionary David Zeisberger.

Pretending to be friendly when they arrived in the evening, Captain Williamson and his militiamen moved quickly, locking the Indian men in one log building, while the women and children were imprisoned in, another. Realizing now that they were in

and live to bear witness to this slaughter.

It is to be noted that this massacre took place some years before the start of the great westward migration and that therefore when this migration finally got under way many Indian tribes of the region, remembering Gnadenhutten, resented the coming of the White Man and the White Man's God. It is also to be noted that the militiamen at Gnadenhutten scalped the

GNADENHUTTEN MASSACRE

danger, the Indians spent the whole night praying.

While the Indians' voices were lifted, the militiamen became more and more intoxicated with whisky they had carried with them. Then, in the misty dawn, they sprang into action with guns, tomahawks, and scalping knives, wantonly murdering all of the colony, except for two Indian boys. Although scalped, these were not so seriously harmed that they could not make an escape

Indians with knives—an operation, it is said, first introduced to America by English settlers when a bounty was offered in colonial Virginia for Indian scalps.

From the very first, the Ohio and Mississippi rivers were the great arteries of travel into the interior country. Neither the men of Marietta nor the Moravian missionaries were the first white men to enter the wilderness region that later became the Midwest. They were preceded by the French, who re-

BLENNERHASSETT MANSION

mained until they were driven out by the British in 1763. When the French flag was replaced by the British, the Ohio River grew in importance as a highway into the western empire.

In those early years, however, the Ohio was traveled mainly by fur traders from the Atlantic seaboard. From the ranks of these traders arose such prominent frontiersmen as George Croghan, Simon Kenton, George Rogers Clark, and Daniel Boone. All of these adventurous trail blazers were familiar to the Indians of the western wilderness long before the arrival of the men of the Ohio Company of Associates. Another frontiersman of the same time and place was Simon Gerty, "The White Savage," who served in the pay of the British during the Revolution and who helped the redskins scalp many an American settler.

While the western country was developing, while the hilly banks of the Ohio re-echoed to the flatboatman's lusty song:

Hi-o, away we go,
Floating down the river
on the O-hi-o,

a dark plot was being hatched on an island in the Ohio River, a conspiracy whose discovery shook the nation. This began when Aaron Burr arrived at Blennerhassett Island, fourteen miles below Marietta, in the year 1806. That was not long after he had served as Vice President of the United States and had killed Alexander Hamilton in a duel. On the island the restless and ambitious New Yorker is supposed to have conspired with Harman Blennerhassett, a wealthy Irishman, to set up an empire in the Southwest.

This plan was about to be carried out, fifteen barges having already been built for the expedition down the Ohio and the Mississippi, when the plot was discovered and Blennerhassett Island was captured. Militiamen destroyed Blennerhassett's commodious and elegant mansion. Although Burr

LORENZO DOW

MIKE FINK

and Blennerhassett were acquitted of a treason charge, they were the subject of much conversation for a long time afterward.

About this time, there traveled through Ohio River settlements a famous pioneer preacher who has almost become legendary since his passing. Riding on a horse, his Jesuslike beard waving in the wind, Lorenzo Dow was an impressive figure as he arrived for a camp meeting. At these gatherings, Lorenzo Dow lifted his voice and soon his backwoods listeners were worked up to a high emotional pitch. It is said that Lorenzo Dow "travelled through the United States from fifteen to twenty times . . . often preaching where a sermon was never heard before." He even introduced the camp meeting into England, but was not so successful when he tried it in Ireland.

Of greater local fame was that king of western flatboatmen, Mike Fink. He is now, in fact, an American folklore hero, as is Johnny Appleseed, and Paul Bunyan. One of Mike Fink's most famous stunts was "shooting the cup." This consisted of shooting a tin cup of whisky off the head of a fellow boatman at thirty yards' distance. But the husky, swearing, whisky-drinking Mike

Fink tried this stunt once too often. He put a hole through the boatman's head instead of through the tin cup and in turn had a fatal bullet hole put through his own head by an enraged friend of the boatman target.

More on the gentle side are the legends centering on that other renowned character of the early Ohio River country, Johnny Appleseed. While Mike Fink was roaring and swearing up and down the rivers, the barefooted Johnny Appleseed, in his tattered clothing and makeshift cardboard hat, wandered quietly from clearing to clearing, planting apple orchards, helping the settlers, and preaching the Word of God. For more than forty years he journeyed over Ohio, Indiana, and Illinois, always carrying a bag or two of seeds. His real name was John Chapman. One legend has it that he had received a good education in his native Massachusetts. Another legend relates that it was a broken love affair that

JOHNNY APPLESEED

BIRTHPLACE OF ULYSSES S. GRANT

caused him to take up the lonely life of a wanderer. Long after his death in 1847, people were reminded of him each spring when pink blossoms came to orchards, and each fall when red apples hung from branches.

Not all of those who came down the Ohio on flatboats, barges, or rafts were Easterners. Many Southerners ferried across the stream and established settlements that later became towns and cities on the Ohio, Indiana, and Illinois shores. It was a Southerner who laid out the now important river city of Portsmouth. Farther down the river is the old village of Neville, named after a Virginian who was granted fourteen hundred acres of land there.

When Neville was a promising settlement, a small boy on a farm not far away stared in wonder at the new steamboats which were then beginning to appear on the Ohio. His name was Ulysses Simpson Grant. The future Civil War general was born in an unpretentious farmhouse here in 1822, and as a boy in this region he watched with great interest the pageantry of the Ohio packets. When Grant was a youngster, however, the Indian menace along the Ohio was a thing of the past. There was no chance of young Grant having an opportunity to take part in the beating up of some Indian boys. But this chance came at an earlier period to a group of five white children. They were out hunting along the Ohio one day when they were captured by a roving band of redskins. Taken to their captors' village, the five white boys were soon the object of ridicule and insult from Indian boys. The white lads stood this as long as they could and then pitched in and attacked. A general fight followed. For a while the elderly braves looked on with amusement, but when the battle got too hot they broke it up.

In 1811 the first steamboat to appear on the river, the *New Orleans,* caused such a stir among backwoods folk that not a few of them thought the clanking river craft may have caused the earthquake which occurred in the Upper Mississippi Valley at

[121]

the time of the *New Orleans'* maiden voyage. This historic vessel was built by Nicholas J. Roosevelt, great-granduncle of Franklin D. Roosevelt, in association with Robert Fulton. Both builders were on board the craft when it left the shipyards at Pittsburgh in 1811 for its first journey down the Ohio and Mississippi rivers. After fourteen days, with an average speed of ten miles an hour, it arrived at its destination. When it attempted to return to Pittsburgh the effort was a failure: its engines were not strong enough for the upstream passage.

This defect was thought to have been overcome when, in 1816, Captain Henry M. Shreve built a stouter vessel than the Roose-velt boat, calling it the *George Washington*. But this newer craft came to a tragic end. On her maiden voyage down the Ohio, just below Marietta, the *George Washington* "blew her boilers," killing eight people and injuring many others. This was the forerunner of many such accidents on the Ohio and the Mississippi.

Because of its strategic location on the river, Cincinnati quickly emerged as a leading metropolis of the Midwest. This city had its beginning in 1788, a few months after the men of the Ohio Company of Associates established Marietta. General Putnam and his carpenters were hardly finished with their stockade at Marietta when

CAPTIVE WHITE BOYS FIGHT INDIAN YOUTHS

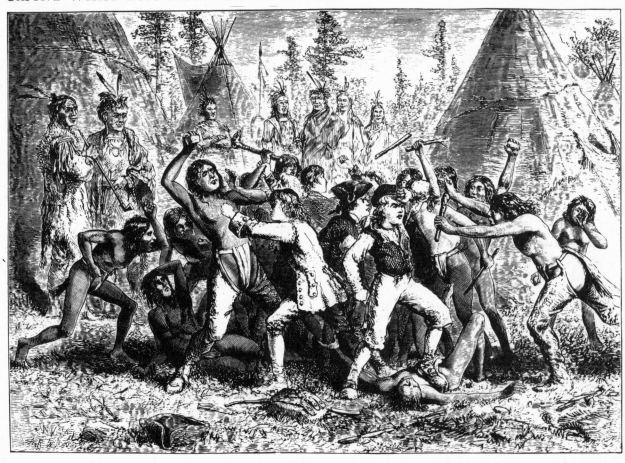

THE *New Orleans*

George Washington EXPLOSION

JOHN CLEVES SYMMES

ANNA SYMMES HARRISON

another flatboat flotilla came down the Ohio and passed the settlement at the mouth of the Muskingum. In command of this flotilla was John Cleves Symmes, a New Jersey land speculator whose daughter, Anna, was to become the wife of President William Henry Harrison.

On Symmes's tract between the Great and Little Miami rivers, below Marietta, the settlement of Cincinnati quickly expanded,

to become eventually the "Queen City of the West." At a time when Chicago was but a small cluster of cabins Cincinnati was a flourishing city, the steamboat capital of the Western country and a center of learning. Here the old South came into contact with the new Midwest. Here came German and Irish immigrants from Europe, sturdy, hard-working men and women who helped to make Cincinnati into an even bigger city

[123]

than before. These immigrants gave Cincinnati a rich, cosmopolitan atmosphere.

Originally, a military stockade called Fort Washington stood on the site of Cincinnati and in command of it was a young Army officer, Captain William Henry Harrison. Around this fort were built the crude log homes of the first settlers. In those early days a pond occupied the place where now stands the city's new nine-story Post Office and Federal Building in the heart of the downtown district.

In 1810, the Queen City of the West contained about four hundred dwellings, a courthouse, and two printing offices. When more steam packets appeared along its water front, Cincinnati developed phenomenally.

Because of its air of prosperity, Cincinnati in the 1840s and 1850s gave the impression that it would become "The Greatest City in America." One of its principal downtown avenues then, Fourth Street, was crowded with the victorias of wealthy merchants, planters from the South, owners of steamboat lines, and the clattering carts of forwarding houses. Here were the elegant Grecian temple of the Post Office and Customs House and the ornate facades of such

CINCINNATI

1802

1810

1846

FOURTH STREET, CINCINNATI, IN 1858

BACKWOODSMEN AND PILOT

well-known establishments as Mitchell and Rammelsburg's furniture store and Shillito's drygoods house.

And down at the Public Landing, as the city's long cobblestoned water front is called, there was a great stir of big white packets arriving and departing, of bales, boxes, and other cargo being hauled over gangplanks by sweating, singing Negro stevedores, and of beery-smelling taverns loud with the voices of steamboatmen. And watching this lively scene on the sunny levee might be a few off-duty pilots or a backwoodsman or two.

Then came the dark days of the Civil War. Among those who took part in the exciting "squirrel hunters'" defense of Cincinnati in the early period of the conflict was the artist-historian Henry Howe, who had for some years been a resident of the

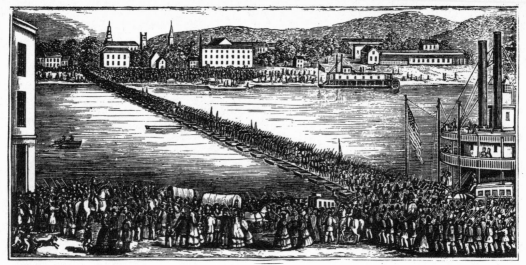

"The Squirrel Hunters"

"Suspension Bridge"

Art Academy (*left*) and
Art Museum, Cincinnati

city. In his *The Times of the Rebellion in the West,* he gives a vivid description of the city's defenders crossing the Ohio River on a makeshift bridge and heading for the interior of Kentucky. "But the . . . most picturesque sight of those remarkable days," says Howe, "was the almost endless stream of sturdy men who rushed to the rescue from the rural districts of the state. These were known as the 'squirrel hunters.' "

This "squirrel hunters' " defense of Cincinnati was successful, for the threatened invasion of the city did not come to pass. With the war over, Cincinnatians resumed their normal way of life and in 1869 built a fine Art Academy. It is still standing. Adjoining it is the Romanesque pile of the Cincinnati Art Museum, built in 1886.

Most visitors to Cincinnati are fascinated by its historic Suspension Bridge, the first such span to be built over the western waters of America. It was begun in 1857 and completed in 1867 and antedated both the Eads Bridge in Saint Louis and the Brooklyn Bridge. Stretching from Cincinnati to Covington, Kentucky, this magnificent structure was designed and built by John A. Roebling.

If many Cincinnatians, on warm Sunday afternoons, enjoyed a stroll on the Suspension Bridge, from where they could see the gaudy white steamboats below on the broad Ohio, just as many found pleasure in those other outstanding sights and institutions of the Cincinnati of an earlier day, the Mount Auburn Inclined Plane, the Zoological Garden, and Highland House. The last was the best known of Cincinnati's pleasure spots in

ZOOLOGICAL GARDEN, CINCINNATI

HIGHLAND HOUSE

MOUNT AUBURN INCLINED PLANE

the 1880s. It was an elaborate German beer garden on top of Mount Adams. Here, on hot summer nights, foregathered thousands of families to drink beer and listen to music. In the summer of 1877, Theodore Thomas brought his orchestra to Highland House and staged concerts there nightly for three weeks. When not enjoying themselves under the trees of Highland House, the German immigrants of the city pursued comfortable, orderly lives in an old neighborhood

CINCINNATI STREET TYPES

"OVER THE RHINE" SALOON

But Cincinnati in the old days was not entirely German. There were almost as many Irish immigrants, and large segments of Southerners and Yankees. Of the latter group, one of the best known and respected was Judge Alphonso Taft, father of the late President William Howard Taft. A sturdy Vermonter, Judge Taft came west to Cincinnati when he was a young man and in time was elected a judge.

On the front steps of Cincinnati's oldest famous house, which, still standing, is now an art gallery, William Howard Taft accepted the Republican nomination for the presidency of the United States. At that time this house was owned and occupied by the presidential nominee's half brother, Charles Phelps Taft, a newspaper publisher. In the years before the Civil War, however, this was the home of Nicholas Longworth I, founder of the great Longworth fortune. Viewing the house today and comparing it with a drawing in an 1858 issue of *Harper's Weekly,* one observes that its fine classic façade is little changed since the days of "Old Nick" Longworth. It was built about 1820.

Not only was Nicholas Longworth a millionaire real-estate promoter but he was also a grape grower of high distinction and his vineyards stretched for miles. He was described as "a friend to artists . . . and very eccentric." Contemporary with "Old Nick" was another prominent Yankee family, the Beechers. The best-known of this clan were the head of the family, Doctor Lyman Beecher, Harriet Beecher Stowe, and Henry Ward Beecher. As a resident of the river metropolis, Harriet Beecher Stowe learned much concerning the miseries of Negro slaves.

Still another prominent family closely as-

known locally as "Over the Rhine." It was a neighborhood of neat homes, beer gardens, turner halls, concert halls, and Teutonic restaurants. In its crowded streets could be heard the calls of the white-coated sausage man. During the cold winter months the saloons of the "Over the Rhine" section were smoky and loud with the chatter of beer waiters.

ALPHONSO TAFT

NICHOLAS LONGWORTH I

LONGWORTH MANSION

sociated with Cincinnati and its vicinity was the Harrison clan. Some thirteen miles down the river from Cincinnati stands the ancient river town of North Bend, identified with two presidents of the United States, William Henry Harrison and his grandson, Benjamin Harrison. Here was located the so-called log-cabin home of General William Henry Harrison at the time he ran for president in the famous "Hard Cider" campaign. Here, too, is his tomb.

Some forty miles north of the Ohio River lies the classical, elm-shaded town of Oxford, the seat of Miami University, one of the oldest institutions of higher learning in the Midwest, at which innumerable Cincinnatians received degrees. Of greater interest than this, however, is the fact those

LESSON IV.

blest	guide	tar'dy	teach'er
learn	wrong	les'sons	school'-boy
haste	i'dler	end'less	knowl'edge

HASTE THEE, SCHOOL-BOY.

1. HASTE thee, school-boy, haste away,
   Far too long has been thy stay;
   Often you have tardy been,
   Many a lesson you 've not seen;
   Haste thee, school-boy, haste away,
   Far too long has been thy stay.

2. Haste thee, school-boy, haste away,
   Join no more the idler's play;
   Quickly speed your steps to school,

PAGE FROM ONE OF McGUFFEY'S
ECLECTIC READERS

LYMAN BEECHER

HARRIET BEECHER STOWE

WILLIAM HENRY HARRISON'S TOMB

HOME OF WILLIAM HENRY HARRISON

renowned American schoolbooks, *McGuf-fey's Readers,* had their birth at Miami University in the early 1830s. While William Holmes McGuffey was a young professor at Miami he wrote the first of his *Eclectic Readers,* illustrated textbooks that shaped the youthful minds of three or four generations.

Serving in early days as a main highway into Ohio, which in 1803 became a state, the Ohio River performed the same task for Indiana during its territorial period and later. Among the first to enter the Territory of Indiana was a group of Swiss immigrants, who founded a river settlement called Vevay, where in time they were producing fine wines. There is no evidence, however, that Edward Eggleston, who, although a non-Swiss, was born and reared in Vevay, ever tasted of the cup that cheers, either during his boyhood or later. But it

was in this backwoods region of the river valley that Edward Eggleston obtained the material for his Midwestern classic *The Hoosier Schoolmaster.* Here he met such mischievous schoolboy types as Hank Banta, who tried one day to entrap the schoolmaster, Ralph Hartsook, into a "plunge bath," only to have the master outwit him, causing Hank himself to fall into the trap.

Farther down the Ohio from Vevay, past Madison and New Albany, there stands, a few miles inland, the village of Corydon, one of the Hoosier State's most historic communities. Surviving here today is Indiana's second territorial capitol and first statehouse, a plain edifice of blue limestone. The capital of Indiana Territory was established here in 1813 after having been removed from Vincennes, and here the new state of Indiana continued to maintain its seat of government until Indianapolis be-

THE PLUNGE BATH

OLD STATE HOUSE, CORYDON

periment failed a few years later, Robert Owen bought the village from Father Rapp and set up a second colony, which he called "New Harmony." Once again the experiment was unsuccessful, and New Harmony became a conventional American town.

After Indiana became a state in 1816, the Ohio River served another new territory, that of Illinois. Here again we have Easterners moving westward on the Ohio in

HARRISON RESIDENCE, VINCENNES

came the capital of the state in 1825.

Of almost similar historic interest is Vincennes, located on the Wabash River not many miles north of the Ohio River. In this ancient French settlement was erected Indiana Territory's first capitol, a building which is in existence today. Another historic landmark of Vincennes is the residence of General William Henry Harrison, built when he first became Governor of Indiana Territory in 1800. In a sense, General Harrison was the "Father of Indiana." On the grounds of his residence there still stands what is left of a venerable walnut tree under which, according to tradition, the Indian chief Tecumseh violently defied Governor Harrison and the American people in general at a meeting in 1811. A year later Tecumseh, on the side of the British, lost his life in the War of 1812.

One early settlement in Indiana that was considerably talked about among flatboatmen on the Ohio River was New Harmony. Located on the Wabash River, just below Vincennes, it was the scene of one of the first religious-communistic Utopias in the Midwest. Here, in 1815, Father Rapp, a German religious leader, established Harmony, centering activities of the colony in his cruciform stone church. When this ex-

flatboats and Southerners moving northward across the Ohio in ferryboats, both groups this time settling in the woods and on the bluestem prairies of Illinois. One of the first ports of entry into this new fertile region was Shawneetown. It was through this gateway that Morris Birkbeck and George Flower brought their group of English farmers in 1818 and established the colony of English Prairie near the present town of Albion, Illinois. Other parties of immigrants came to the new Illinois country and soon they were going beyond Shawneetown, drifting farther down the Ohio River, getting closer each year to its confluence with the great Mississippi.

But in this region just below Shawneetown there was danger for rivercraft. This menace was not due to snags, shallows, or any other natural object, but arose from the presence there of a man, Samuel Mason, a bloodthirsty river pirate who had his lair in Cave-in-Rock on the Illinois side of the Ohio River. The unscrupulous Mr. Mason and his gang of freebooters raided and robbed flatboats on the Ohio for many years.

About this time, an energetic Saint Louis merchant, John G. Comegys, decided to buy land and lay out a city on the narrow Illinois peninsula at the junction of the Ohio and Mississippi rivers. He gave it the name of "Cairo," apparently believing the site to be similar to that of Cairo, Egypt. Although Comegys' project remained a "paper city," due to his early death, the name Cairo continued in existence for a later town founded there in 1837, giving rise to the popular name of "Egypt" for almost all of southern Illinois. Cairo soon

FATHER RAPP'S CHURCH

became an important steamboat center.

Apparently not a very prepossessing city when Charles Dickens visited it in 1842, Cairo is said to have been the inspiration of the nightmarish City of Eden in *Martin Chuzzlewit*. By the end of the Civil War, however, Cairo could boast of an average of three thousand steamboats docking annu-

TECUMSEH DEFYING GENERAL HARRISON

[133]

CAVE-IN-ROCK

CAIRO

ally. With the coming of railroads into the western country, Cairo became a manufacturing center. And east and west beyond its levee walls, glistening under a hot summer sun like quicksilver, move the stately waters of two of the world's greatest rivers, which, during most of the nineteenth century, formed the crossroads of inland America.

OLD FRENCH TOWNS

THE FIRST Anglo-Saxon settlers of
what is now the Midwest found rem-
nants of a white civilization that had lived
in scattered towns and villages. These were
communities established by the French in
the years when France, by right of discovery, conquest, and settlement, held sovereignty to the entire Mississippi Valley.
Stretching from Quebec to New Orleans,
it was too vast a region, however, for them
to colonize thickly.

In its prime, New France remained a
wilderness, with here and there a fur-trading station, a military post, or a Jesuit mission, or sometimes all three of these combined in one community. When France lost
this huge empire to England at the end of
the French and Indian Wars in 1763, the
habitants, a contented, easygoing class,
chose to stay in their colonial villages on

the Mississippi and other rivers. In time
they were absorbed in the tidal wave of
Anglo-Saxon immigrants.

If these *habitants,* as well as *seigneurs,
curés, coureurs de bois, voyageurs,* and
other colorful French types of the early
American wilderness, have long since
passed from the scene, some of the places
they established are still in existence and
retain their original French names and a
faint aura of Gallic origin. One of these
is Detroit (originally *Place du Détroit,*
Place of the Strait). Other cities and towns
in Michigan that began as French missions
or trading posts are Sault Sainte Marie,
Saint Ignace, Mackinac, Mackinaw City,
and Monroe. In Wisconsin there are Prairie du Chien, Fond du Lac, Green Bay, Eau
Claire, Portage, and La Crosse.

On the Illinois side of the Mississippi,

one may find Cahokia, Prairie du Rocher, Renault, Fort de Chartres, and what is left of Kaskaskia. Here there are many architectural relics and even habits of speech and decorum that still express plainly eighteenth-century Creole culture. In Illinois, too, there are such later French settlements and towns as Bourbonnais, Sainte Anne, and Nauvoo. And in Indiana there is Vincennes, while Ohio has its Gallipolis ("City of the Gauls"). Far to the north, in Minnesota, the city of Duluth is a survival of the French régime.

Saint Louis began as an outpost of New France. In the "Show Me" state there is also Saint Charles, originally French. Of all the Midwestern cities and towns of French origin, none is of greater interest to us of today than Sainte Genevieve, just below Saint Louis in Missouri. Here is a town that not only remains almost as it was more than two centuries ago but in which many descendants of its first colonial French families still live. Probably the most interesting landmark in this age-old town is the Jean Baptiste Vallé House.

One of the earliest of the black-robed French missionaries to visit the wilderness of the mid-continent region was Father Marquette. On a June day in 1673, accompanied by Indian guides, Father Marquette and Louis Jolliet discovered the Upper Mississippi River.

This historic event occurred some three miles below the site where later was founded Prairie du Chien, second oldest town in Wisconsin. A few years after Father Marquette passed this way, a group of Frenchmen set up a fur-trading post here. Incidentally, Father Marquette did not consider himself above physical labor. Like the "Black Robes" who were to come after him, he took his turn at the paddle, helped with the cooking, and did his share

VALLÉ HOUSE

[137]

PASSING WATERFALLS

MARQUETTE AND JOLLIET DISCOVER THE UPPER MISSISSIPPI

FATHER MARQUETTE

DEATH OF FATHER MARQUETTE

of the work in making camp at nightfall.

On their first voyage down the Mississippi in 1673, Father Marquette and Jolliet went as far as the mouth of the Arkansas, at which point they were convinced that the Mississippi flowed into the Gulf of Mexico. Although the Spanish explorer Hernando De Soto was the first to discover the Mississippi, more than a hundred years earlier, it remained for Marquette and Jolliet to reveal that the Mississippi was a great link between the headwaters of the Saint Lawrence River and the Gulf of Mexico.

At the mouth of the Arkansas, Marquette and Jolliet might have been killed by hostile Indians had it not been for a symbolic gift which the priest displayed to the natives. As the Frenchmen glided along in their canoes, they were approached by a large log craft containing nine fierce-looking savages. When these savages showed unmistakable signs of hostility, Father Marquette stood up in his canoe and displayed a finely wrought pipe of peace, which had been given to him by an Indian chief on what later became the Iowa side of the Mississippi. On seeing this object, the sun-worshiping savages extended the hand of welcome. Afterward, Father Marquette found these natives to be in possession of axes of steel, probably as a result of contact with Spanish colonists of the Southwest.

But Father Marquette was not strong enough for the rough life of the wilderness. He soon became ill from his labors. "Two years longer," says Benson J. Lossing in *Our Country,* "Marquette labored among the barbarians of Chicago, when he crossed to the eastern shore of Lake Michigan. Suffering from mortal sickness, and conscious that his death was near, he passed along

INDIAN COUNCIL AT SAINT MARY'S FALLS

that shore in his canoe . . . until it entered a small stream which bore his name for a long time afterward. They carried him tenderly ashore, and laid him upon the leaves in the shadows of the forest. He told them, with joy, that he was about to die, but requested them to leave him alone while they should unload the canoes; and promising to call them when his end should be nigh. He did so very soon. Then he asked for some holy water which he had prepared, and taking a crucifix from his neck, placed it in the hands of one of his companions and desired him to hold it constantly before his eyes while he lived. With clasped hands he then pronounced aloud the profession of his faith, and soon afterward he died."

Before undertaking his first voyage down the Mississippi, Father Marquette was in charge of a Jesuit mission at Sault Sainte Marie, perhaps the first town to be settled by the French in what is now the Midwest. The first white man to visit this site was Etienne Brulé, who came in 1618 and who thought this might be the long-sought Northwest Passage to China. In 1668, a mission was founded here with Father Marquette in charge.

It was not until 1671, however, that the French established official sovereignty over this mission. On a May afternoon agents of the French Government held a Grand Indian Council under the trees at the Falls of Saint Mary's (Sault Sainte Marie). While chiefs of tribes from the Mississippi River, the Saint Lawrence River, and the Red River of the North sat about and smoked calumets, officials announced to them that they were now being placed under the protection of the French King, who had taken formal possession of Canada and the Northwest. Then several Jesuit mis-

BURNING OF FATHER BRÉBEUF AND FATHER LALLEMAND

sionaries addressed the Indians, explaining to them the meaning of the cross. The ceremonies were concluded when, bowing before a large cedar cross, the whole company chanted a seventh-century Church hymn.

At first, however, French explorers and missionaries encountered resistance from some of the Indians. Fathers Brébeuf and Lallemand were burned at the stake. But their deaths and the death of Father Marquette were not in vain, for they had planted the seeds out of which grew missions, villages, and eventually cities, like Sault Sainte Marie, or "The Soo," as it is familiarly known. When a canal and lock were built here in 1855, The Soo was still something of a frontier town, with Indians, half-breeds, and French-Canadians crowd-

PRINCIPAL STREET OF SAULT SAINTE MARIE

ing its wide, dusty streets. Among these residents were many who made a living by portaging freight around Saint Mary's Rapids. This group objected to the building of the canal and lock. Once, when a breach occurred in the embankment of the canal, most of the residents of Sault Sainte Marie refused to help repair it. If it had not been for the speedy assistance of some sailor volunteers, the breach would have caused great damage.

Within a few steps of Saint Mary's Locks there still stands the old home of the great Indian authority, Henry Rowe Schoolcraft, the first official Indian Agent at The Soo in the 1820s. In this rambling frame house, Schoolcraft penned some of the books on Indian life and customs that later inspired Longfellow to write *The Song of Hiawatha.*

Not far from Sault Sainte Marie may be found one of the oldest and best known vacation spots in the Midwest, Mackinac Island, a historic and picturesque bit of pine-shaded land in the wide blue Straits of Mackinac. An early French missionary, Father Claude Jean Allouez, spent the winter of 1670-1671 on the island, preaching to the Huron Indians. Originally settled by *coureurs de bois* and *voyageurs,* Mackinac Island later was occupied by the British and in 1793 it was surrendered to the American Government. It was reoccupied for a time by the British during the War of 1812 and later returned to the Americans. Dominating the little white waterside town of Mackinac, where horse-drawn carriages and bicycles are the only means of transportation, is old Fort Mackinac, surviving from the War of 1812.

UPPER ENTRANCE

SAULT SAINTE MARIE CANAL

LOWER ENTRANCE

[143]

HOME OF HENRY ROWE SCHOOLCRAFT

In addition to this fort, the mile-long Grand Hotel overlooking "The Straits," and the ancient buildings of the John Jacob Astor fur-trading station, Mackinac Island offers an unusual natural wonder, the Arched Rock, a rock bridge suspended almost 150 feet above the surface of a near-by beach and, according to Indian tradition, shaped by giant fairies as a gateway onto the island.

Green Bay is the oldest town in Wisconsin and also was originally settled by the French. The explorer Jean Nicolet claimed this region for France in 1634. It was inevitable that this trading post should develop into a city. Situated at the southern extremity of a great bay, on the pine-clad

HARBOR AT MACKINAC ISLAND

[144]

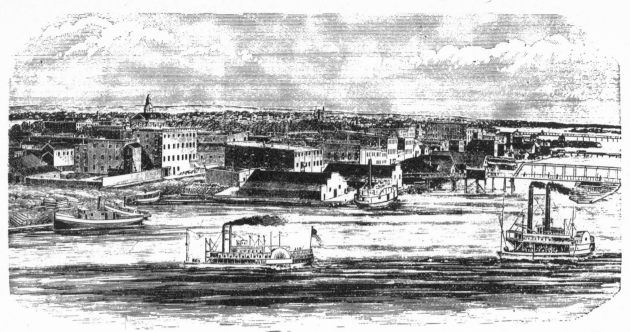

GREEN BAY

ARCHED ROCK

western shore of Lake Michigan, Green Bay early became a halfway station on the water routes of New France.

Surviving today at Green Bay is an ancient house, built by a French fur trader, Joseph Roi, called "The Tank Cottage," after a later owner, Nils Otto Tank. It is widely known as Wisconsin's oldest dwelling house.

Because of its strategic location, Green Bay was defended from the start by French colonial troops, who had built Fort La Baye here. When this region became American at the end of the Revolution, the Federal Government erected a new fortification here, calling it "Fort Howard." An old hospital and the surgeons' quarters are all that remain today of Fort Howard. During the closing decades of the nineteenth century, Green Bay was an important lumbering center. At that time, many descendants of the town's early French settlers were still

REVEREND ELEAZER WILLIAMS

dians of the region for a good many years.

Ascending the Fox River, one comes eventually to that very historic Midwestern spot known anciently as "The Portage." Here (now Portage, Wisconsin) most of the early French explorers and missionaries, and later the *voyageurs* and *coureurs de bois,* carried their canoes overland for a mile or two until they reached the Wisconsin River, on which they paddled to the Mississippi. The first to do so were Father Marquette and Louis Jolliet. As portaging here was difficult and exhausting, many *voyageurs* made it their custom to pitch camp after a crossing, in most cases using their canoe as a form of shelter. Here, after a hearty meal and seated before a blazing

Voyageurs' CAMP

alive and very active in community life.

Associated with the pioneering French days of Green Bay and the valley of the Fox River was a mysterious character, the Reverend Eleazer Williams, thought by some to have been the Lost Dauphin of France. The Reverend Mr. Williams lived in a log house (which is still in existence) near Green Bay after having preached to the In-

THE PORTAGE

fire, they relaxed, played cards, told stories, and made plans for the next day.

Early in the nineteenth century, however, a plank road was laid at the Portage over which ox teams hauled freight and passengers at the rate of fifty cents per hundred pounds. One of the first to engage in such traffic was Pierre Pauquette, a French Canadian who had earlier served as an Indian scout and as an agent of John Jacob Astor's fur company. When the Americans came and formed a settlement at the Portage, there was built here for their protection Fort Winnebago, one of the first officers of which was young Lieutenant Jefferson Davis, afterward President of the Confederacy.

PIERRE PAUQUETTE

PRAIRIE DU CHIEN
IN 1835

FORT WINNEBAGO

After passing the Portage, the French fur traders journeyed down the Wisconsin River to the Mississippi and then up that river for three miles to Prairie du Chien. A busy trading center during pioneer times, Prairie du Chien was the seat of Joseph Rolette, otherwise known as "King of the Fur Traders." Rolette's *voyageurs* brought blankets, food, and firearms and these were

CAHOKIA

given to the Indians in exchange for furs. The river village was a colorful, boisterous place, with *voyageurs* and *coureurs de bois* strolling about dressed in buckskins and bright scarves and wearing earrings and bracelets. Among them mingled stolid-faced Indians, their heads decorated with gaudy feathers. In the 1830s, Hercules L. Dousman was to make a fortune at Prairie du Chien as agent for the American Fur Company, and his elaborate great house is now perhaps the principal sight of this Mississippi River town.

Several hundred miles directly north of Prairie du Chien stands the important Minnesota city of Duluth, at the head of Lake Superior. Seeing this city today, with its extensive ore docks, its railroad yards, and its manufacturing plants, one may little realize that Duluth began its existence as a remote French trading post. This station was established in 1678 by Daniel Greysolon, Sieur Duluth.

The French continued to move southward from the Great Lakes region, founding missions and trading posts. The largest group of French villages grew up in what was known as "The American Bottom," an area of fertile river flats on both sides of the Mississippi above and below Saint Louis.

History records that a feud among missionary priests attended the founding of Cahokia, first of the French villages to be established in the American Bottom. In 1699, Father Jean François Buisson de Saint Cosmé and several other priests of the Seminary of Foreign Missions built a chapel at Cahokia in which they began preaching to the Indians. A group of Jesuit missionaries arrived shortly afterward and

KASKASKIA

RUINS OF FORT DE CHARTRES

PRAIRIE DU ROCHER

CARONDELET

challenged the right of the Seminarists to engage in missionary work in that region. Determined to show their prior jurisdiction, the Jesuits went to work on a chapel of their own. Finally, one of the Seminarists went to France to seek settlement of the feud between the two religious orders in the American wilderness. In 1701 it was decreed that the Seminarists could remain in Cahokia while the Jesuits were to retain their jurisdiction over the rest of the Mississippi Valley.

The rise of Saint Louis and East Saint Louis, five miles above Cahokia, caused the decline of Cahokia, at one time a county seat for almost all of Illinois, including Chicago. Still in existence, although but a mere crossroads hamlet, Cahokia retains numerous landmarks of the days when French *habitants* lived there, among them the Church of the Holy Family, the courthouse, and the Jarrot Mansion.

A few miles south of Cahokia was Kaskaskia, second white settlement in Illinois and that state's first territorial capital. Here the Jesuits set up a mission and from this grew the settlement. This historic village was washed under the waters of the Mississippi River at the close of the nineteenth century. In the late 1830s there was in the town a seminary for young ladies, conducted by nuns of the Order of the Visitation. A large proportion of the inhabitants were of French origin and retained French manners and customs, which, however, gradually gave way to the influence of immigrants from other sections of the country.

Although Kaskaskia is a "sunken village," there survives from it the old Pierre Ménard Mansion, which, because it was

SAINT CHARLES

built on a bluff, escaped destruction in the floodwaters. Completed in 1802, this French-colonial-style dwelling was the home of Pierre Ménard, a French-Canadian fur trader who became the first Lieutenant Governor of Illinois. Not far.from the Ménard home is located the old Kaskaskia Cemetery.

If one were riding in a *calèche* from Cahokia to Kaskaskia during the French régime, one would very likely stop for rest and refreshment at Fort de Chartres, which was France's "Gibraltar of the Mississippi Valley." Here, during the middle decades of the eighteenth century, France maintained a stronghold that protected most of her settlements along the Mississippi and in the Illinois Country, as well as her black-robed missionaries and her far-roaming agents in the fur trade.

Prairie du Rocher, a quiet, ancient village at the foot of a rocky bluff, six miles from Fort de Chartres, was founded about 1722 by some of the many French families who were left stranded in the region after the bursting of John Law's "Mississippi Bubble" in 1720. John Law had obtained from France a charter to colonize the Upper Mississippi Valley, promising to bring six thousand whites and three thousand

TYPICAL EARLY FRENCH HOUSE

PONY CART

CARRYALL

CALÉCHE

Negroes into the region. When this "bubble" burst with a roar that was heard on two continents, many of the French families who had been lured to the area remained there.

Meanwhile, there grew up across the Mississippi an *habitant* village named Carondelet, out of which emerged Saint Louis. Originally, however, Carondelet was a Spanish settlement, established at the time Spain owned all territory west of the Mississippi.

Some twenty miles northwest of Saint Louis, on the Missouri River, stands the small city of Saint Charles, which has a sizable Germanic strain in its population. In the beginning, this city was French. Although a French-Canadian fur trader,

Louis Blanchette, settled here in 1769, it was not until 1787 that the village was formally established by Auguste Chouteau. In after years, Saint Charles served for a time as the Territorial and first State capital of Missouri and one of its principal historic sights is the old capitol buildings.

In all of the French settlements and villages, life centered in the home. Most of the houses of the *habitants* were of log construction, but instead of being built of horizontal logs, like the later cabins of the American frontier, they were sided with vertical logs. They were characterized by a high-peaked gabled roof which extended outward to form a porch, or *galérie,* at the front, or on all four sides, of the house, this latter an importation from the French West Indies. At

[153]

one end of the dwelling, or at both ends, might be stone chimneys, which made possible fireplaces of generous proportions. Built rather close to the village street and behind a whitewashed picket fence, the average French colonial house stood in the midst of a spacious yard. The interior of such a house would be simply but comfortably furnished, with chairs and tables often handmade, and on the walls the visitor might find religious pictures, or perhaps a crucifix. In some of the wealthier homes of New France one could dine off imported plate, or play a game of billiards.

For sustenance, the French colonists depended entirely on the products of their own farms. As a rule, farming was done in the same manner as along the Saint Lawrence, on a partly individual and partly collective plan. At planting time in the spring, all of the families worked in *Le Grand Champs,* or "The Big Field," each family laboring in the long, narrow strip which it owned in this field, a strip that usually extended from the river's edge to the end of the tract. A simple wooden plow, with a metal share, was used, pulled by a yoke of oxen. Not far from the village was reserved another tract of land, the "commons," over which cattle and hogs could roam.

Once the spring crops were planted, little cultivation was necessary and the habitants indulged in a leisurely mode of life, enjoying numerous *fêtes* and making fre-

SUMMER EVENING IN A FRENCH VILLAGE

[154]

quent social calls. Of the various horse-drawn vehicles among the colonists, the most familiar was a primitive two-wheeled cart. Sometimes this cart contained a chair or two for the comfort of riders, but most often a buffalo robe was used to sit on, or to provide protection in cool weather. The gentry frequently rode in the elegant two-wheeled *calèche,* a vehicle brought down from Quebec. During the snowy winter months, most all of the families used a car-ryall, a graceful wooden sled.

WEST OF THE RIVER

WESTWARD, ever westward, moved the people of the East. During the expanding years of the nineteenth century, they kept coming into the western country, at first in canoes and on flatboats, then in covered wagons and stagecoaches, and finally on steamboats and railroad trains. At the end of the century, the immense American frontier no longer existed. Now the people of the East, and the people from the Old World, too, had completely settled the stupendous, fertile, well-drained valley of the Upper Mississippi. Now they had reached the semiarid plains at the foot of the Rockies. This was the last and perhaps the greatest phase in the pioneer development of the Midwest. Out of this phase, in what was once the old Louisiana Purchase, emerged the far-flung agricultural states of Missouri, Kansas, Ne-

braska, North Dakota, and South Dakota.

In the beginning, those who ventured westward beyond the Mississippi went up the Missouri River in canoes, following in the wake of the Lewis and Clark Expedition. Afterward, some of the pioneers stopped on the banks of the wide Missouri, staked out claims, and induced others back East to join them, and soon settlements and river towns were flourishing. But others continued westward in covered wagons. Sometimes there were long trains of these wagons, moving slowly in a cloud of dust across the treeless prairie country toward a land that lay beyond the Missouri River. In the earliest days of this migration, Saint Louis was an outfitting station for both overland wagons and river flatboats.

Despite this activity, Saint Louis did not become the capital of Missouri when the territory was admitted to statehood in 1821. In seeking a capital site, the State's first General Assembly had its eye on some point along the Missouri River. At first it was decided to establish the capital at Côte Sans Dessein, near the mouth of the Osage River, but when land speculators flocked here, the assemblymen gave up this plan. Thus it was that Jefferson City, a mere riverside landing, offering nothing more than a mission and a foundry, was chosen. In time a two-story brick capitol building was built on a bluff overlooking the river. In its earliest days, Jefferson City grew but slowly, and citizens of other towns clamored for the removal of the capital to their communities.

After Governor John Miller, eager to keep the capital at Jefferson City, built the State Penitentiary there in 1836, the town was assured of its political primacy. Development of the village was further stimulated with the coming of the Pacific Railroad in 1855.

At the time Jefferson City became the state capital, there was a crossing on the Missouri River many miles westward known locally as William Jack's Ferry. A few Southerners began to settle on the south bank of the river there and thus came into being the town of Lexington, named after Lexington, Kentucky. Here was fought, years later, American history's other "Battle of Lexington." It was an intense, three-

JEFFERSON CITY IN THE 1850S

LEXINGTON, MISSOURI

KANSAS CITY, 1850

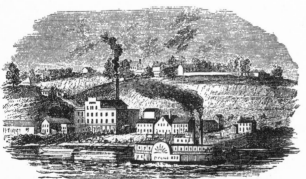

[157]

HANNIBAL BRIDGE

SAINT JOSEPH

day battle of the Civil War, between the Confederate troops of General Sterling Price and the Union soldiers of Colonel James A. Mulligan. The latter group was known as "The Irish Brigade" and was composed mostly of Chicagoans of Irish birth or parentage.

Westward from Lexington the Missouri River meanders over the level countryside for many miles, finally coming to a point where it turns northward and heads for the plains of Nebraska. Because of this "Great Bend," there grew up here Kansas City. On arrival at the Great Bend, immigrants had to disembark and continue the westward journey on land. When John Calvin McCoy set up a store near the Great Bend to supply the wants of those about to head westward, other merchants were attracted to the spot, business grew, a town was laid out called Westport. In time this town became an outfitting station for wagon trains setting out on the Santa Fe and Oregon trails. Thus Kansas City was born.

As a gateway to the Western Empire, Westport was a lively, colorful frontier town. The historian Francis Parkman wrote: "Westport is full of Indians, whose little shaggy ponies were tied by dozens along the houses and fences. . . . Whiskey circulates more freely in Westport than is altogether safe in a place where every man carries a loaded pistol in his pocket."

Although Missouri River steamboat traffic at Kansas City declined with the coming of the railroads, this did not affect the life of the city. The change proved a blessing, marking the beginning of a new and greater era in the city's history. After the completion of the Hannibal and Saint Joseph Railroad Bridge, "K.C." became even more important, extending its zone of influence all the way to the Texas Panhandle. More and more wheat trains came from the fields of Kansas and Nebraska.

Steaming northward from Kansas City during prerailroad days, a river packet would next call at Saint Joseph, an old Missouri town that is famous for other reasons than the fact that Jesse James was shot and killed here. Saint Joseph played an important role in the Gold Rush of '49, serving as a jumping-off place for gold seekers on their way to California. We are told that between April and June, in 1849, almost fifteen hundred prairie schooners passed through the dusty streets of the frontier town and, after crossing the Missouri, headed for the Far West. Here, too, in 1860, was established the famous Pony Ex-

PIONEERS ATTACKED BY INDIANS

a circle around which were posted guards.

Among some of the strange sights they saw were prairie-dog "towns" on the plains of Nebraska or Kansas. From a distance, such a town has the appearance of motionless wavelets spread out for miles. On closer approach, one sees the wavelets to be small mounds, arranged rather symmetrically like streets. As the observer comes closer, reddish, squirrellike animals perched on top of each "house" utter sharp cries of warning and quickly disappear into their little hillocks. Here, in underground chambers, where they live and rear their young, the prairie dogs wait until all danger is past. Then, one by one, they come out of their holes, once more mount their hillocks, and gaze at the retreating form of the observer.

An even stranger sight than a prairie-dog town was observed for a time on the Nebraska prairie in 1860. Evidently intended to outdo the prairie schooner, this strange sight was a "wind ship wagon," an

PRAIRIE DOG TOWN

press, which carried mail to Sacramento.

After leaving such end-of-the-world points as Kansas City or Saint Joe for the long, weary journey to the Far West over lonely prairie trails, early pioneers were oftentimes attacked by roving bands of Plains Indians. To protect themselves against these attacks, these homeseekers would, at nightfall, arrange their wagons in

WIND SHIP WAGON

overland vehicle deriving its motive power from sails.

Almost as many "movers" on their way to the wide grasslands of Kansas and Nebraska passed through Iowa as through Missouri. At Iowa City, pioneer families gazed in awe at the Hawkeye State's new stone capitol building, begun in 1840. Designed in the prevailing classic mode, this building served as Iowa's capitol until 1857, when the state capital was removed from Iowa City to Des Moines. Thereafter, the old capitol became the administration building of the State University of Iowa. It is still standing.

Iowa also saw segments of the great Mormon migration. Wagon trains of Mormons pitched temporary camps in Iowa on the way to their new "State of Zion" at Salt Lake City, Utah. Such a temporary camp was established in 1856 at Fort Des Moines by about six hundred men, women, and children of the Mormon faith. Once more on their way westward, these Mormon families formed into single file and traveled on foot, each family pulling a handcart.

In the early years of the nineteenth century, before Omaha existed, wagoners and horsemen crossing the Missouri River at the future site of Council Bluffs, Iowa, would have come to a little frontier settlement called Bellevue. Founded about 1805, long before Nebraska became a territory, Bellevue was for years a trading post of John Jacob Astor's fur company. Later the government set up an Indian Agency here and afterward the Presbyterian Church conducted a mission house for tribesmen of the western plains.

It was not until after 1860, when Congress passed the Homestead Law, giving each settler on western lands 160 acres at twenty-five cents an acre provided he lived on his tract for five years, that Omaha began to take on the aspects of a western boom town. Through this "gateway" passed thousands of immigrants, both native- and

OLD STATE HOUSE, IOWA CITY

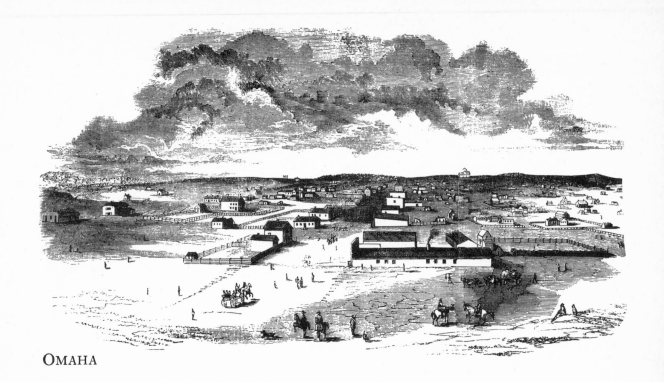

OMAHA

BELLEVUE

MORMONS MOVING WEST

BUFFALO HUNT

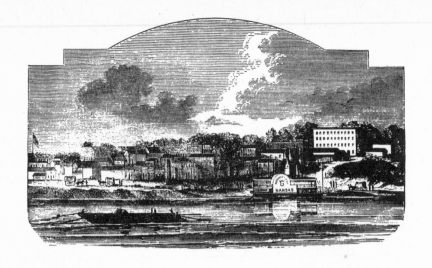

LEAVENWORTH, KANSAS,
IN THE 1850S

BRIDGE AT TOPEKA

foreign-born. This movement was greatly accelerated after Omaha became the eastern terminus of the Union Pacific Railroad in 1867.

Not only were larger numbers of immigrants than before attracted to it, but the city became a supply depot for "dude hunters" from the East, sportsmen in search of buffalo, wolves, and other animals. But it is extremely doubtful whether any "dude hunter" from the East could have engaged in buffalo hunts such as were staged by hardy plainsmen in the early days. Feats of

this kind required not only courage and skill but a more than usual amount of manly strength. Plainsmen oftentimes lost their lives or were permanently injured while attempting to come to grips with the powerful, shaggy bison. One plainsman who attained fame, as well as a nickname, in this activity was Buffalo Bill Cody. It was as a supplier of buffalo meat to railroad-construction crews in Nebraska that William F. Cody first came to the attention of the world.

Nebraska Territory and the Territory of

Kansas were both born out of the fateful Kansas-Nebraska Act of 1854. In the latter territory occurred bloody battles between antislavery and proslavery factions, a vicious warfare started by the act which allowed the new territories to decide the slavery question for themselves. This bill brought a rush of proslavery Southern immigrants to Kansas Territory. One of the first towns they founded was Leavenworth, centering it around old Fort Leavenworth, which had been built in 1827 by Colonel Henry Leavenworth and had served to protect wagon trains on the Santa Fe Trail. Another town established by proslavery elements was Atchison.

There was just as big an influx of anti-slavery Northerners, including the fiery Abolitionist John Brown. The Northerners set up the towns of Lawrence and Topeka. Located on the Kansas River and in earlier days a stopping point on the old Oregon Trail, Topeka soon was a lively, growing town as more and more Northerners arrived, entering it over a long wooden bridge that here spanned the Kansas River. When Kansas Territory was admitted into the Union as a free state in 1861, Topeka became its capital.

Still standing in Topeka today and that city's most revered historic landmark is Constitution Hall, a rude log building in which the free state of Kansas was born. Here, on an October day in 1855, delegates

KANSAS TERRITORY CONSTITUTIONAL CONVENTION

[165]

LECOMPTON

representing the antislavery faction drew up a constitution and formed a territorial government, expressly forbidding Negro slavery in the new Territory. This govern-ment was declared unconstitutional by an already established proslavery administration. Thus began the warfare between Southerners and Northerners in Kansas

TROOPS ARRIVING AT CONSTITUTION HALL

Territory which made that region widely known as "Bleeding Kansas" and which was one of the direct causes of the Civil War. When "The Topeka Government" attempted to convene again in Constitution Hall, it was prevented from doing so by United States troops.

At the time this episode occurred, the capital of the proslavery territorial government was at Lecompton. Here, on the second floor of the Masonic Hall, was framed "The Lecompton Constitution," which permitted slavery in the new territory. A year later, when Northerners gained control of the Legislature, this constitution was repudiated. And afterward, when submitted to a vote, it was refused by most of the settlers of the Territory. But this did not end the border warfare between proslavery Missourians and antislavery Kansans,

which continued up to, and during, the Civil War.

During the war, Northern families in Kansas lived in continual fear of roving bands of Southern guerrillas. They did not know at what hour of the night such a band would invade their home, murder male members of the family, and set fire to their dwelling. One of the most notorious of the guerrilla leaders was William Quantrell. Just after daylight on the morning of August 20, 1863, Quantrell and about three hundred of his men quietly stole into Lawrence, long an antislavery center, and killed many of its citizens, practically all of whom were unarmed. Then, after looting the town, Quantrell and his guerrillas applied the torch and that evening the once flourishing Kansas town of Lawrence was a smoking mass of ruins.

GUERRILLA ATTACK ON UNION HOME

[167]

CATTLE ARRIVING AT DODGE CITY

But out of this bloody border warfare, and out of the much wider and more terrible conflict of the Civil War, emerged the free state of Kansas, as well as an entire nation free of slavery. It was after the Civil War, and when the West was expanding rapidly, that the Sunflower State had its beginnings as a cattle and wheat-producing region. Soon Dodge City, out on the sunny plains of southwestern Kansas, came into being as the cow capital of America. During its heyday as such, Dodge City was a riotous western town, its bare dusty streets crowded with cowboys, buffalo hunters, bullwhackers, and muleskinners. And when the great "drives" came up from Texas, the wide streets and environs of Dodge City became runways for thousands of cattle, a huge mass of milling, bawling Texas longhorns kept in line by the cracking whips of fast-riding cowhands. From Dodge City, the cattle were shipped to such meat-processing centers as Kansas City and Chicago.

At the time Kansas was emerging as a cattle center, so too was it coming to the fore as a wheat-producing region. At this period, also, Dakota Territory began attracting national attention as a new wheat area, one promising even larger crops than the Sunflower State. So great had interest in Dakota Territory become, that when President Rutherford B. Hayes made a transcontinental tour in 1878 he saw to it that his journey included a trip through the vast, waving wheat fields of the Northwest.

On arrival in the territory, President Hayes was taken to one of the largest farms in the region, the Dalrymple Farm. Located in the valley of the Red River of the North, some eighteen miles west of Fargo, the Dalrymple Farm embraced a total of one hundred thousand acres. For convenience of operation, this huge tract was divided into farms of two thousand acres each, with a superintendent in charge of each farm.

"At the time of his [President Hayes'] visit," said a contemporary periodical, "four steam-threshers were at work, and upwards of fifty teams were in sight, plowing for the next year's crop. The President and party, escorted by Mr. Dalrymple, spent two hours riding on the farm, witnessed the threshing and plowing, and freely expressed admiration and astonishment at the magnitude of the operation."

When North and South Dakota were admitted to the Union in the latter years of the nineteenth century, the Midwest attained nearly complete settlement. Here was a region that, stretching from the Alleghenies to the Rockies, had been founded and developed within the comparatively short span of one hundred years. With towering cities, wide-spreading farms, humming factories, interlacing highways, and leafy white towns in all directions over the region today, there must be pride indeed in the hearts of many Midwesterners yet with us who can look back to a time when their section was but vacant prairie, shadowy forest, or barren shore. Now old, white-haired, and sunning themselves on the porches of comfortable residences where once stood log cabins or mere shacks, these aged pioneers delight their grandchildren and great-grandchildren with stories of their experiences and adventures as Founding Fathers of the Midwest.

ACKNOWLEDGMENTS

WHILE engaged in this task at the Newberry Library, I had the generous assistance of the librarian, Dr. Stanley Pargellis, who placed a cubicle at my disposal. I was also greatly aided by those on Dr. Pargellis' staff—Mr. Joseph Wolf, head of the division of local history and genealogy, and his assistants, Mrs. Ellen Chase and Miss Marcia Thayer; Mrs. Ruth Lapham Butler, custodian of the Edward E. Ayer Collection; Mrs. Gertrude L. Woodward, custodian of the Rare Book Room; John T. Windle, director of the General Reading Room; and Mr. Robert H. Brannan, administrative assistant to Dr. Pargellis. There was, too, the unstinting time and effort given by my wife, Marion Neville, to a careful reading and editing of the manuscript of this book, for which I hereby express my deepest appreciation.

At the library of the Chicago Historical Society, where I also did considerable research work, I was given much assistance not only by the director, Mr. Paul M. Angle, but by the librarian, Miss Margaret Scriven, and her staff of aides.

The selection from *A History of Chicago* by Bessie Louise Pierce is quoted by permission of The University of Chicago Press.

The sources of the pictures are as follows:

Abraham Lincoln, by Charles Carleton Coffin
American Magazine of Useful and Entertaining Knowledge
Ballou's Pictorial Drawing Room Companion
Chicago by Day and by Night
Chicago, by Eugene Seeger
Chicago: Her History and Her Adornment, by Mabel McIlvaine
Commercial and Architectural Chicago, by G. W. Orear
Das Illustrirte Mississippithal, by Henry Lewis
Farm Ballads, by Will Carleton
Farm Festivals, by Will Carleton
Forty Etchings, by Basil Hall
Frank Leslie's Illustrated Newspaper
General History of the State of Michigan, by Charles R. Tuttle
Gleason's Pictorial
The Graphic
Harper's Weekly
Historical Collections of Ohio, by Henry Howe
Historical Collections of the Great West, by Henry Howe

History of Brown County, Wisconsin, by Bella French

History of Chicago, by A. T. Andreas

History of Cook County, by A. T. Andreas

History of Kansas City, by William Griffith

History of the Early Settlement of the Mississippi Valley, by Firmin A. Rozier

The Hoosier Schoolmaster, by Edward Eggleston

Illinois Central Railroad pamphlet

The Illinois Country, by Clarence Walworth Alvord

Illustrated Chicago News

An Illustrated History of the State of Indiana, by Charles R. Tuttle and Dewitt C. Goodrich

Indiana Gazetteer

Iowa as It Is in 1855, by Nathan H. Parker

The Land Owner

Leading Events of Wisconsin History, by Henry E. Legler

The Life of Abraham Lincoln, by Ward H. Lamon

Life of Lincoln, by Joseph H. Barrett

Life on the Mississippi, by Mark Twain

The Lincoln Album, by C. M. Biggers

Lloyd's Steamboat and Railway Guide

McGuffey's New Third Eclectic Reader

Memorials of a Half-Century, by Bela Hubbard

Missouri as It Is in 1867, by Nathan H. Parker

Newberry Library

Our Country, by Benson J. Lossing

Our Whole Country, by Henry Howe

Pioneers in the Settlement of America, by William A. Crafts

Prairie Farmer

Stories and Sketches of Chicago, by J. B. McClure

The Story of Chicago, by Joseph Kirkland

The Story of Sault Ste. Marie, by Stanley Newton

Thrilling Incidents in American History, by John Warner Barber

Through the Flames and Beyond, by Frank Luzerne

The Times of the Rebellion in the West, by Henry Howe

The Valley of the Mississippi, by J. C. Wild

INDEX

[174]

[175]